HISTORICAL DEVELOPMENT OF THE
UNIVERSITY SYSTEM OF GEORGIA

Historical Development of the University System of Georgia: 1932-2002
Second Edition

———————

Cameron Fincher
Regents Professor
   of Higher Education and Psychology
(Director 1969-1999)

Institute of Higher Education
The University of Georgia
Athens, Georgia

Preface to the Second Edition

The first edition of this brief book discussed the historical development of the University System of Georgia from 1932 through 1990. No effort was made at that time to write a comprehensive history of the Board of Regents, the various institutions that are now units of the University System, or the innumerable public issues and policy decisions that have been instrumental in the growth and expansion of public higher education within the state of Georgia. And no such effort has been made in writing a second edition that discusses the continuing development of the University System from 1990 through the year 2002. Thus, the second edition is an extension of the first edition and not a revision. A conscientious effort has been made to correct errors that were printed in 1990, and attempts have been made to replace inept phrases with a better choice of words.

As stated in the first edition, the historical development of the University System is more intelligible when discussed in terms of its institutions, programs, services and activities. To that end, many other stories have been carefully avoided. There has been no desire or intent to write about politics or personalities; that is another story altogether and one that would distract greatly from many significant and meaningful efforts to develop a comprehensive system of public higher education in Georgia. Neither is the story one of the Board of Regents, its individual members, and its policy-making procedures. That, too, is another story to be told by others.

Special care has been taken to "control" references to funding, financing, and budgeting. The search for adequate funds is a never-ending struggle in higher education and once introduced into a discussion, funding (like politics) dominates everything else that follows. Enough is said about annual budgets to show that funding is important, and will always be a matter of intense concern. Enough has been said also to show that institutions of higher education can and do survive under financial adversity.

Another related matter that has been avoided is the legal issues of the past forty-five years. Legal issues and judicial process are often more dominant than finances and politics. Legal proceedings, in particular, lead to eventual resolutions of conflict but not to the solution of educational problems. After the judication of conflict it is virtually impossible to trace cause and effect relations in the midst of so many concurrent events and unanticipated outcomes.

This book would be more interesting if it could explain how public policy issues are resolved and how major policy decisions are made. Regrettably that story must be avoided like politics and funding, but not for the same reasons. Observation and study of "the process" will suggest that policy decisions are seldom made in public. The majority of policy decisions are seldom a matter of mere proposal and approval; such decisions are not disclosed in recorded minutes, published statements, or written policy manuals. Neither is a policy decision merely the exercise of personal power or influence, a matter of who decided what on which day! With respect to the public and institutional policies discussed here, it has been difficult enough to peg major policy decisions with a date.

Why then a book on the University System's historical development and *not* a history of the University System of Georgia? The reasons are fairly clear; the development of institutions, programs, and services in a complex, multi-purpose, statewide system of public higher education is never a matter of specific events, decisions, and actions. For the most part, such development is an extended process in which varied responses are made to the stimulus of public demands and expectations. The development of institutions, in particular, implies an internal differentiation and integration of structures and functions that often follow a schedule of their own. No one creates a university (or university system) by signing a charter, enacting a law, amending the constitution, or rendering a majority vote. The creation of such institutions is a developmental process that takes many years and the concerted efforts of many people. Thus, there are excellent reasons to believe that "historical development" is the appropriate term to designate what this book is all about. The development of the University System of Georgia began several years before the Reorganization Act of 1931, and it continues long after the Board of Regents attained constitutional status and authority.

Because of such reasoning, readers will find a pronounced emphasis on survey reports, committee recommendations, the work of outside consultants, and various public documents such as annual reports. Taken one at a time, they are a tedious form of literature; taken together they tell a story that all Georgians should appreciate. Dry and dusty reports often tell us what was missing "at the time," what was needed but not supplied, and what the next "stage of development" might possibly be. Many of these reports were written by observers with the best of intentions, but far removed from the pressures of policy and decision making. As a result, they were often able to see more clearly what needed to be done and how to do it. At other times, of course, they were professionally right but historically wrong.

The University System thus has grown and developed in response to public demands and expectations that changed as "the times changed." Institutions of higher education have been closed, merged, reorganized, planned, established, and appraised as social, economic, political, and cultural conditions changed for "better or worse." Programs of instruction, research, and service have prospered or struggled with changes in public and private support. *And* the units of the University System have responded with programs and services as public demands and expectations have changed with national, regional, and state trends.

Writing the last three chapters of the Second Edition has been both a challenge and a pleasure! To select and to summarize the major features of the Regents strategical planning process has been quite difficult because so much was accomplished in a relatively short period of "institutional time." The development of mission statements and their concrescence is not a feat easily described and quickly told. And the coalescence of thirty-four institutional visions as "a unity of the whole" is a story that must be told later.

Having witnessed the University System's growth and development since 1946, I was especially pleased to observe the University System's remarkable advancement during the past ten years (1992-2002) and its national recognition as the nation's fourth largest statewide system of public higher education. Those of us who remember the early 1950s and the aspirations of smaller institutions to gain greater status can testify to the amazing accomplishments of the past forty years—and to the fortunate circumstances that sustained both economic growth and progressive leadership.

In their responsiveness to changing demands, the colleges and universities of the University System have exceeded most reasonable expectations. In many respects and from many different perspectives the University System is the state of Georgia's most remarkable achievement and the finest thing that Georgians have ever done for themselves. As a statewide system of public higher education, the University System is exemplary; its progress has often been uneven and irregular, but its progress has been continuous and its development reflects a commitment to intellectual, technological, and cultural progress that is often missing in other areas of human endeavor. Georgians, like residents of other states, are occasionally inclined to boast; in the University System of Georgia they have accomplished something in which they can take genuine pride.

Cameron Fincher
December 4, 2002

Acknowledgements

A book of this kind is necessarily the outcome of many years of reading, observing, listening, discussing, and writing. In dedicating the first edition to the memory of Thomas W. Mahler (1917-1990) who, upon retirement as director of the Georgia Center for Continuing Education, gave me his collection of the Regents' Annual Reports, I tried to acknowledge my professional indebtedness to a colleague who was quite influential in my professional career.

In writing the second edition I am indebted to the Board of Regents, members of the chancellor's staff, and many others for the encouragement, assistance, and opportunities I have been given to "tell the story" of the University System's continuing growth, development, and maturity during the past twelve years. Members of the chancellor's staff were particularly helpful on numerous occasions. As a result of their cooperation and their interest in the University System's historical development, I gained a better appreciation of the crucial role the chancellor plays in the University System. Thus, it seems most appropriate to dedicate the second edition to the chancellors whose leadership and commitment have been essential in the University System's historical development:

Harmon W. Caldwell (1949-64)

S. Walter Martin (Acting, 1964-65)

George L. Simpson, Jr. (1965-1979)

Vernon Crawford (1979-1985)

H. Dean Propst (1985-1993)

Stephen R. Portch (1994-2001)

In their various years of service each chancellor has contributed significantly and substantiably to the continuing development of higher education throughout the University System and to the intellectual and cultural welfare of Georgia citizens. I am especially indebted to readers of the first edition who expressed their personal interest in the University System and provided additional information about its development. Wherever I turned for information, advice, or assistance, I found an interest in the University System's rising status and national recognition. Acknowledgments of the highest order are due GEORGIA CROWN for financial assistance in meeting printing costs, INFORMATION TECHNOLOGY OUTREACH SERVICES for statewide maps, and the University of Georgia Printing Department for printing the book. As in the first edition, their cooperation and contribution reflects the generous interest of others in the University System's history.

In similar manner, it is appropriate to acknowledge the various forms of assistance given in the preparation of the second edition for publication. In the second edition—as in the first— Mrs. Susan Sheffield has again rendered excellent service in preparing camera-ready copy. She has also supervised the preparation of the maps depicting institutional growth and location, and she has served conscientiously as liaison with the University Printing Department. Mrs. Cathy Elrod has rendered excellent assistance in typing and retyping chapters, paragraphs, and sentences that did not always improve with the author's revision. Doug Mann proofed and double-checked many pages that needed a critical eye and a better choice of words.

Cameron Fincher
December 4, 2002

We state emphatically that it is not our purpose to aggrandize any institution, without due regard to all of the others. It is, however, our plain duty to mold the institutions in the University System into an Educational System, in fact, as well as in name. It must comprise a group of separate institutions, under common control . . ."

—1932 Annual Report

Contents

List of Figures

CHAPTER ONE
Reorganization and Coordination: 1932-1943

> To understand any belief, any ideal, any custom, any in-
> stitution, we must examine its gradual growth from
> primitive beginnings to its present form. The character of
> an individual and the civilization of a nation are the re-
> sult of a long development. . . . Time and history are of
> fundamental importance.
>
> John Herman Randall, Jr.
> *Making of the Modern Mind*, 1926

The University System of Georgia has developed gradually and unpredictably since its inception in the early
1930s. The System began in the interest of economy
and under conditions that were extremely adverse for education.
As the System has developed, it has overcome one adversity only
to be set back by another. Nonetheless, the life history of the
University System has been an appreciably steady, gradual, and
continuous progression to its current status as the nation's fourth
largest statewide system of public higher education.

The authority and responsibility of the Board of Regents have
evolved in the midst of many legal, political, economic, and social
difficulties. The Constitution of 1877 (adopted in the post-recon-
struction era) provided for schooling in the "elements of an
English education only" and for "donations" by the general
assembly to the University of Georgia. As a result of legislative
short-sightedness, the development of both secondary and higher
education within Georgia was severely hampered. No provision
for state-supported high schools was made until the early years
of the 20th century when amendments to the 1877 Constitution
allowed the general assembly to delegate the levy of taxes for
"educational purposes" to counties (*Orr, 1950*).

The movement for a centralized governing board for all public
institutions of higher education began in the 1920s as part of a

public demand for the reorganization of state government. Specific mention of a board of regents was made as early as 1919 when Governor Hugh Dorsey (1917-1921), as chairman of the budget and investigating committee, stated:

> We are decidedly of the opinion that it would be in the best interest of our higher institutions of learning if a small Board of Control or State Board of Regents should displace the army of trustees now appointed largely by reason of political support. (p. 15)

In 1922 Governor Thomas W. Hardwick (1921-1923) commissioned a study of state government with specific mention that the state was "board-ridden, commission-ridden, and trustee-ridden." The General Assembly took no action on the recommendations of the consultants hired by Governor Hardwick, but public support for simplification and reorganization gained momentum five years later. In 1927 the Georgia League of Women Voters, the Institute of Public Affairs at the University of Georgia, and the Institute of Citizenship at Emory University actively supported reduction of the state's ninety-plus agencies to twelve or fourteen departments. At that time the University of Georgia had 331 trustees for its various branches (Gosnell, 1936).

The report of a state survey committee, appointed in 1925 by Governor Clifford Walker (1923-1927) and chaired by C. Murphey Candler, stated that "possible friction or rivalry between the higher institutions and some duplication of work could be eliminated, and much better results for all obtained, if there were one Board of Trustees or Regents . . ." (p. 8). The committee added that proper safeguards should be involved in appointments and the alumni of no one institution should dominate.

In 1929 the Georgia Commission To Simplify and Coordinate the Operations of Governmental Departments was appointed by Governor L. G. Hardman (1927-1931) and chaired by Ivan Allen, Sr. The commission recommended a department of state government to be known as the "Board of Regents of the University System of Georgia" (p. 23). The University System should consist of the University of Georgia and all its branches. The plan for reorganization was drawn up by Chairman Allen, Hooper Alexander, and Cullen Gosnell; the accompanying legislative bill was drafted by a committee of the Atlanta Lawyers' Club (Gosnell, 1936).

The bill for reorganization was defeated in the House by a vote of 109 to 81, but the essential features of the bill were revised by a legislative committee appointed by Speaker Richard B. Russell, Jr. and chaired by Hugh Peterson who had been a member of the Allen Commission.

When Russell was elected governor (1931-1933), he repeated his pledge to reorganize state government. The Reorganization Act of 1931 quickly followed and with the abolishment of 53 state boards, commissions, and bureaus the powers previously vested in 27 boards of trustees were consolidated under a single Board of Regents *(Saye, 1948)*.

The University System of Georgia became a legal reality on August 28, 1931 when Governor Richard B. Russell, Jr. signed an act of the General Assembly "To Simplify the Operations of the Executive Branch of State Government." The Board of Regents was officially organized on January 1, 1932, the first day of its existence, and consisted of eleven members appointed by the governor who served as an *ex officio* member. Prominent members of the first board were Cason Callaway, Martha Berry, Richard B. Russell, Sr., George C. Woodruff, and Philip Weltner. The first elected chairman of the Board of Regents was W. D. Anderson of Macon and the first appointed chancellor was Charles M. Snelling, former president of the University of Georgia. Philip Weltner was elected vice-chairman and Earle Cocke, Sr. was appointed secretary-treasurer.

The first Board of Regents thus consisted of eleven members, one each from the ten congressional districts and one member at large who served at the pleasure of the governor. Members of the Board were appointed by the governor (with consent of the Senate) for four terms. They elected their own chairman and were authorized to select a secretary.

The Regents inherited from the various preceding boards serious financial problems. For the years 1929-1931, the Regents inherited outstanding debts of $1,074,415 and 26 institutions whose locations were "known only to a few" and whose operations were "known to no one person or group" (*1932 Annual Report*).

The institutions and agencies for which the new board was responsible were an unbelievable array of senior and junior colleges, A&M schools, and agricultural experiment stations. From the various boards of trustees, the Regents inherited three university-level institutions located in Atlanta, Athens, and Augusta; five senior or four-year colleges located in Athens, Milledgeville, Statesboro, Tifton, and Valdosta; three junior colleges at Cochran, Dahlonega, and Douglas; eight district A&M schools (or their variants) in Barnesville, Bowden, Carrollton, Clarkesville, Granite Hill, Madison, Monroe, and Powder Springs; three colleges for blacks in Albany, Forsyth, and Savannah; and two agricultural experiment stations in Griffin and Tifton.

As shown in Figure 1, these various agencies had been scattered about the state in response to local needs, as perceived in the past, and in tune with the political pressures of the era in which they had been established. Only two of the agencies were located north of Atlanta and only one was located on the Georgia coast; none were located in the northwest and southwest corners of the state. Three of the institutions were located in Athens alone: the University of Georgia (1785), the Georgia State College of Agriculture and the Mechanic Arts (1872), and the State Teachers College (1895). The colleges for agriculture and education began as separate institutions and later became a branch of the University with their own presidents and trustees. Their complete integration within the University of Georgia would not be complete for eighteen more years.

Each of the 26 institutions began as a hopeful solution to the state's educational problems. The A&M schools were established in 1907 and 1908 as district high schools to meet the needs of rural areas. The schools were located in each congressional district *as* branches of the State College of Agriculture and *with* trustees as representatives of the included counties. Their programs were a mixture of manual labor and secondary schooling that was superceded by the growth of public high schools and by passage of the Smith-Hughes Act of 1917 that provided funds for institutions in agriculture, home economics, trades, and industrial subjects. By the mid 1920s the A&M schools had outlived their purpose and seven were converted to colleges by the state legislature. Descendants of four A&M schools would become Georgia Southern, Georgia Southwestern, South Georgia, and Middle Georgia colleges.

The three colleges for blacks began as the Georgia State Industrial College (1890) in Savannah, the Georgia Normal and Industrial College (1917) in Albany, and the State Teachers' and Agricultural College (1922) in Forsyth. The latter college would

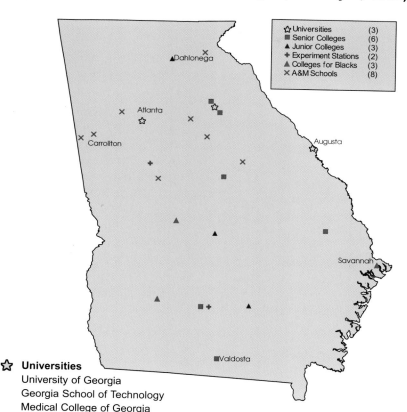

FIGURE 1
Original Institutional Composition of the
University System of Georgia (January 1, 1932)

☆ Universities	(3)
■ Senior Colleges	(6)
▲ Junior Colleges	(3)
✚ Experiment Stations	(2)
▲ Colleges for Blacks	(3)
✕ A&M Schools	(8)

☆ **Universities**
University of Georgia
Georgia School of Technology
Medical College of Georgia

■ **Senior Colleges**
Georgia State College of Agriculture
   and the Mechanic Arts
Georgia State Teachers College
Georgia State College for Women
Georgia State Woman's College
Georgia State College for Men
South Georgia Teachers' College

▲ **Junior Colleges**
North Georgia College
Middle Georgia College
South Georgia College

✚ **Experiment Stations**
Georgia Experiment Station
Georgia Coastal Plains Experiment Station

▲ **Colleges for Blacks**
Georgia State Industrial College
Agricultural, Industrial & Normal School
State Teachers & Agricultural College

✕ **A&M Schools**
4th District A&M School
7th District A&M School
8th District A&M School
9th District A&M School
10th District A&M School
Bowden State Normal
   and Industrial College
State Agricultural & Normal College
Georgia Industrial College
The Georgia Vocational & Trade School

Information Technology Outreach Services, Universtiy of Georgia

be consolidated in 1939 with the Fort Valley High and Industrial School (1895) to become Fort Valley State College. The two experiment stations were outgrowths of the Hatch Act of 1887 and in 1932 they were independent state agencies with federal funding.

To cope with its 26 disparate institutions and their debts, the Board of Regents moved quickly to obtain $20,000 from the General Education Board for a comprehensive survey by "disinterested expert educators and economists." The objective of the survey was to make the University System "more efficient from an educational viewpoint and more economical from a taxpayer's point of view" *(1932 Annual Report)*. The funded survey began in May 1932 and was concluded in February 1933. Members of the survey committee were: George F. Zook, president of the University of Akron; Lotus D. Coffman, president of the University of Minnesota; Charles H. Judd, dean of education at the University of Chicago; Edward C. Elliott, president of Purdue University; and George A. Works, professor of higher education at the University of Chicago (and chairman). The members of the survey committee were well-respected educators and the survey they conducted was typical of national efforts to study and to improve the general condition of education beyond the high school.

Among the Regents' many accomplishments in their first year were the requirement of surety bonds for institutional deposits in local banks, the consolidation of all insurance for the separate institutions, the discontinuance of institution-owned automobiles, and completion of its first year *without* borrowing money. Despite receiving only 86 percent of its state appropriations for 1932, the Board reduced its indebtedness to $702,502.

Constructive measures were taken to integrate the three separate Athens institutions into one. Farms and dairies were combined, and all dining halls and dormitories were placed under one management. Policies were established whereby faculty salaries would be decreased proportionately to reductions in state appropriations. For 1932 this meant a 14 percent reduction in faculty salaries which was in addition to other reductions imposed to balance institutional budgets. The total reduction in institutional operations for the year was $507,739.

Policies were established whereby heads of institutions would handle all personnel grievances and settle other internal difficulties. The Regents would hear complaints only when other remedies had been exhausted and when appeals were "reduced to writing." The Regents heard only two appeals in 1932, both of which resulted in sustainment of the president's decision.

One institution, the 10th District A&M School at Granite Hill, was closed in 1932. Foremost among the Regents' recommendations to the governor was authority to "consolidate institutions, suspend and/or discontinue their operation, merge departments, inaugurate or discontinue courses, abolish or add degrees." The reorganization of institutions would be less drastic if done by the Regents instead of the General Assembly. Given such authority, the Regents would eliminate institutions offering only high school work and remove secondary schoolwork from other institutions (with the exception of the three black institutions).

Also sought by the new board was a single appropriation from the state *and* the authority to allocate and/or distribute such funds as the Regents saw fit. Some institutions had funds in excess of their necessities while others were in want. The state legislature did not have time to ascertain institutional needs, but the Regents did. In recommending a reduction of state appropriations in 1933 (from 1.9 million to 1.5 million dollars) the Regents demonstrated awareness of the state's financial depression but added that they could not operate on the lesser budget without the requested authority to re-organize.

Other recommendations made by the first Regents were:

(a) a fiscal year beginning on July 1st and ending the following June 30th;

(b) annual appropriations according to the new fiscal year; and

(c) a special appropriation of $100,000 for repairs to buildings. (The special appropriation for repairs was the only recommendation not honored by the state legislature.)

In closing its first annual report, the Regents stated their commitment to an "Educational System, in fact, as well as in name" and their encouragement of "diversity of educational effort because of the diversity of human needs." The Regents, however, did not "subscribe to the idea of multiplying courses and taking on new fangled educational ideas because some great university, with millions of dollars of endowment funds, is experimenting in these fields." The Board did subscribe to "a sense of obligation to their State" on the part of students and the necessity of local pride giving way to the best educational interests of the whole state (*1932 Annual Report*).

A New University System

With the additional powers authorized by the state and the recommendations of its prestigious survey committee, the Board of Regents created in 1933 a strengthened system of senior and junior colleges. Relinquishing most of their responsibility for secondary schoolwork, the Regents closed A&M schools in Carrollton, Powder Springs, Madison, and Clarkesville, plus the Vocational & Trade School at Monroe. They discontinued high school coursework at South Georgia Teachers' College (in Statesboro), North Georgia, Georgia Southwestern, Middle Georgia, and South Georgia colleges but continued such work at the institutions in Savannah, Albany, and Forsyth.

State support for the Bowden State Normal & Industrial College was discontinued when West Georgia College (a junior college) was established in Carrollton. The Georgia State College for Men in Tifton was abolished and replaced by Abraham Baldwin Agricultural College. Senior college work was also eliminated at North Georgia, giving the state a total of eight two-year colleges (six for whites and two for blacks).

Seven institutions were classified as four-year institutions and included the newly merged University of Georgia (including the agricultural college and the normal school), Georgia Tech, Georgia State College for Women (Milledgeville), Georgia State Woman's College (Valdosta), South Georgia Teachers' College (Statesboro), the School of Medicine (Augusta), and Georgia State Industrial College (Savannah). Creating the Evening School of Commerce (or Division of Adult Education of the University System of Georgia), the Regents added an eighth four-year institution and, with the two agricultural experiment stations, brought the total number of University System units to eighteen (*1933 Annual Report*).

In his 1936 annual report Chancellor S.V. Sanford announced that the reorganization of the University System had been completed and added that "no further changes are considered necessary." The 1936 annual report was the fifth from the Regents, the first to Governor E. D. Rivers, and the second to be written by Chancellor Sanford. It was also the first annual report to include photographs of buildings on the various campuses. Chancellor Sanford overlooked the role of the New Deal in the University System's "economic recovery" and addressed the more pressing educational issues facing the state's system of public higher education. Among the many educational needs recognized were:

(a) more attention to guidance and counseling,

(b) a graduate school of "high standing,"

(c) graduate work for teachers,

(d) the demand for trained men and women in social service (or rural sociology),

(e) more adequate libraries (including the best library of Georgia history and literature in the country).

The First Works Report

The reorganization of higher education in Georgia was significantly influenced by the survey committee report written by George A. Works and submitted in 1933. Among the recommendations *not* followed by the Regents, however, were several concerning the composition of the Board. The membership of the Board of Regents, according to the survey committee, should consist of ten or twelve members appointed to longer terms (either ten or twelve years) and should not include the governor as an *ex officio* member. Regents appointed to the Board should represent the state's economic and cultural interests but *not* its congressional districts. The reasoning of the consultants was explicit: the chief executives should not appoint a majority of the Regents or exercise undue influence. Citing the National Association of State Universities, the survey committee pointed out that "the theory (of *ex officio* membership) is thoroughly unsound, the practice is even worse."

The Regents did follow (eventually) the recommendation that the chancellor, and *not* the chairman of the Board, should be the chief executive officer. They were more reluctant, however, in appointing an executive secretary "properly trained in educational and statistical techniques, [and] charged . . . with the necessary duty of assembling, analyzing, and interpreting the regular and special reports of the operations of the several branches of the University System" *(1933 Annual Report).*

Also followed was the recommendation that "responsibility for work at the high school level" be placed on local school authorities. Ignored was a similar recommendation that the "local character of the junior college and the functions which it has in the program of education point to the desirability of the transfer of the junior college to local communities" *(p. 29)*. Referring to a commission report in California, the survey committee acknowledged a national trend for junior colleges as "the last stage of the upper or secondary school period of common schooling" and stated that as junior colleges became an integral part of secondary education, they should be placed under the State Board of Education.

Although the 1933 survey report recommended the reduction of the University System of Georgia to no more than nine or ten units, the composition of the System became six senior institutions, six junior colleges, three historically black institutions, and two experiment stations. Yielding to local pressures, the Regents resorted to such actions as closing Georgia State College for Men in Tifton (a four-year institution) but opening Abraham Baldwin Agricultural College (a two-year college). In similar manner, the Regents transferred General University Extension from the University of Georgia and the Evening School of Commerce from Georgia Tech to an independent unit that first became the University System of Georgia Center, then the Atlanta Division of the University of Georgia, and eventually Georgia State University.

The Second Works Report

In 1940 the Board of Regents again obtained funds from the General Education Board for "a re-study" of conditions in the University System. Dr. George A. Works was employed as director of the survey and his report, delayed until 1943, gives an overview of higher education in Georgia on the eve of World War II. Drawing heavily from his earlier report, Works documented the limited support given public higher education in the depression years and defined the problems and issues that would confront the University System when the national emergency was over.

The limited support given public higher education was shown by a record of ten consecutive years in which the state funds received by the University System fell short of the funds appropriated by the General Assembly. Not until 1940 did the University System receive its full state appropriation of $1.75 million. Failure to implement the recommendations of the earlier Works Report was shown by repeated recommendations:

    (a) to strengthen the chancellor's professional staff through the appointment of a vice chancellor responsible for fiscal and budgetary matters;

(b) to adopt uniform budgetary forms and procedures for the separate units and a complete, consolidated budget for the University System;

(c) to separate purchasing for the University System from the office of the state purchasing agent; and

(d) to develop a more serviceable committee structure to assist the chancellor in his systemwide administrative duties.

In reviewing the status and support of the three state-supported colleges for blacks, Works reaffirmed the earlier recommendation that "a more liberal policy of support" was needed. The need for better support was shown by the low faculty salaries in the black colleges—and the survey committee asked that "more ample state support" be put as "the first and most important recommendation of this section" of their report. Significantly, the second Works Report recommended:

(a) the material strengthening of undergraduate, general education programs at the three institutions;

(b) the strengthening of professional training in agriculture, home economics, and teacher education; and

(c) the provision of scholarships for graduate and professional study.

Within these recommendations the report noted that Atlanta University "is in a position to meet the needs of students in certain fields of graduate and professional study" and asked the chancellor, along with the three presidents of the black institutions, to prepare a list of such institutions acceptable to the Board of Regents.

In the area of student services, the Works Report suggested that progress had been made—but again, significant progress had not been made. To meet such lack of progress, the survey staff recommended the appointment of "a coordinator of student personnel services" but hastened to add that "an Assistant to the Chancellor and a Business Manager" should be given precedence. Noting that the University System had appointed a university examiner to develop "through tests and measurements a competent program of student personnel and guidance" (*p. 92*), the survey staff endorsed the need for "inquiry and experimentation" in student personnel work and specifically pointing out the importance of diagnosing reading disabilities, poor study habits, and other learning difficulties that students may have had. Further recommendations included:

(a) the development of a statewide testing program in the high school;

(b) a special study of student financial aid;

(c) the "cooperative interpretation" of the University System through better publicity and conferences of high school principals and counselors;

(d) better housing for students; and

(e) a uniform system of application blanks, student record forms, etc.

Graduate education and research were treated in the second Works Report in a chapter entitled "Miscellaneous Problems." Graduate instruction was offered exclusively at the University of Georgia and Georgia Tech. Discussed at greater length in the same chapter were the problems of the University System of Georgia Center, the only unit of the University System not accredited by the Southern Association of Colleges and Schools. Among the problems discussed by the Works Survey Committee were:

(a) the dubious offering of three years of coursework in the liberal arts at the center;

(b) the heavy reliance on part-time instructors drawn from the business community;

(c) excessive teaching loads; and

(d) the institution's sole dependence on student fees for income.

The concluding chapter of the second Works Report dealt with the finances of the University System and depicted in detail the financial support given public higher education in Georgia. Virtually all data were for 1940-41, the last year of operations before the nation's entry into World War II.

The figures told a discouraging story. With a per capita income of $297, Georgians could look only to Mississippians, Arkansans, Alabamians, and South Carolinians as making less. Yet, Georgians spent only 39 cents each on higher education while their sister states spent at least 53 cents (Mississippi) and as much as 84 cents (Alabama). As the largest unit of the University System, the University of Georgia enrolled the full-time equivalent of 3,901 students but had only $1.08 million to spend on their education. West Georgia, the smallest unit, had only $70,582 to spend.

The cost per student-credit-hour in the University System ranged from $6.15 at the University of Georgia to $2.25 at the

University System Center. From UGA's per-student-credit-hour cost, 49 cents was spent on administration and general overhead; $1.13 was spent on plant operations and maintenance; 43 cents was spent on the library; leaving $4.10 for instruction. Each of the junior colleges spent less than $2.00 per student-credit-hour.

Full-time-student expenditures ranged from $277 at UGA to $101 at the University System Center. Only the University of Georgia, Georgia Teachers, and Georgia State Woman's College in Valdosta, among the senior institutions, spent as much as $10 per student for books. Within the University of Georgia, instructional costs ranged from $17.50 per student-credit-hour in education to $2.28 in journalism.

The survey staff strove to demonstrate the merits of unit costs in financing and budgeting. They recommended that each institution submit its annual budget to the Regents in terms of unit costs, using the full-time-student equivalent as the basis. They made a particularly strong case for increased support by pointing out that the actual appropriation to higher education had decreased since the University System was created, having been reduced 40 percent in a single year (1938-1939). Appropriations were reduced despite an increase of 70 percent in student enrollment (from 8,035 students in 1933-1934 to 13,736 in 1940-1941).

The final recommendations made in the second Works Report called for increased salaries for administrators, faculty, and staff; increased support for graduate instruction; more liberal support for the Division of General Extension and the University System of Georgia Center; "much more ample facilities . . . and provision for instruction" for the higher education of blacks; and the addition of $50,000 to funds for miscellaneous purposes. If granted, the suggested budgetary increases would come to $600,000 and have raised the University System's then current income to a total of $2.5 million.

Recurrent Themes and Issues

The early years of the Board of Regents and the two Works reports are reviewed at length because: (1) they depict the difficulties of establishing a statewide system of public higher education under extremely adverse conditions, and (2) they identify many recurring problems, issues, and concerns in public higher education. Each of these problems, issues, and/or concerns were considered by later Boards and survey committees, and each was dealt with in terms of the conditions and situations prevailing at the time.

Recurring educational issues were found in: (1) agriculture, (2) engineering, (3) business, (4) teacher education, (5) minority access, and (6) general education. Organizational and governance problems were found in: (7) the geographical distribution of institutions and programs, (8) financing and funding, (9) student services, (10) the mission of two-year colleges, (11) programs for part-time, adult students, and (12) the training of physicians and nurses. Each of these issues or problems had a direct bearing on the quality of postsecondary education and on the public's changing expectations for education beyond the high school.

Agriculture: Both Works reports noted the University System's need to integrate resident instruction, extension services, and applied research in agriculture. The need for integration of these functions was identified as the most important issue faced by the Board of Regents in the field of agriculture. As for veterinary medicine, it was recommended that its professional curriculum at the University of Georgia be discontinued. This recommendation for such unification was eventually resolved in 1951, but the nature and extent of agricultural programs continued to be a recurrent theme.

Engineering: In 1940 the most pressing problem in engineering education was the inadequacy of its funding. Georgia Tech's annual expenditures were barely one million dollars and the per-student instructional cost of $270 was regarded by experts as "wholly inadequate." The institution's role as something more than a local or state institution was noted, and the state's failure to provide adequate facilities was deemed contrary to the state's desire to exercise control. Specifically noted in the second Works Report was the question of presidential longevity and replacement by someone "widely recognized for his standing in science or engineering as well as for his qualification as an administrator and leader" (*p. 76*).

Business: The Board of Regents' reasons for closing Georgia Tech's School of Commerce and transferring its Evening School to an independent Department of Adult Education were: (1) the state could not afford two competing schools of commerce, and

(2) strong schools of commerce could not be developed indepen-
dently of "high-grade work in economics, history, and government"
(p. 11). The Regents thought it advisable to develop "a real center
of adult education in Atlanta" by transferring the University of
Georgia's Department of General University Extension to Atlanta
to work in conjunction with the newly formed Evening School
of Commerce. Similar reasoning would be used in later years in
the establishment of Georgia State University.

Teacher Education: The preparation of public school teachers as
a responsibility of institutions of higher education and the difficulties of cooperation among accrediting agencies, schools of
education, state boards of education, and governing boards were
an obvious *and* pressing issue. By 1943 the University System was
"well equipped with buildings and equipment" to train teachers
for public schools, but adequate funds were not yet available "to
hold or to attract the type of teachers needed in our university
system and our public school system" *(Annual Report for 1943-1944)*.

Minority Access: In his 1943-1944 annual report, Chancellor
Sanford did not address the recommendations of the second Works
Report concerning the status and support of the state's historically black institutions. In the midst of World War II, he discussed
the difficulties and benefits of specialized training programs
for military personnel, the decreases in civilian students, and the
prospects of the GI Bill and other changes on postwar education.

General Education: The influence of World War II on higher education was seen in the mobilization of college campuses to assist
in the war effort. Chancellor Sanford, in 1944, was convinced that
"technical education on the college level will have a permanent,
and not a subsidiary place in the educational program" *(p. 47)*.
Neither the nation nor the community could afford the "tragedy
of undeveloped talent."

Geographical Distribution: Despite war-time restrictions, the
excessive duplication of programs and courses was a matter of
concern in 1943-1944. The University of Georgia, according to its
president, offered too many courses and the faculty was urged to
study curricular offerings and to eliminate courses of dubious
value. Chancellor Sanford rejected the "ancient idol" that the
best colleges were those that offered "the greatest number of
subjects or the greatest variety of courses" *(p. 38)*.

Financing and Funding: Student *per capita* expenditures at the University of Georgia were $116, the lowest among state universities of the region. At Georgia Tech, *per capita* expenditures were $90, as compared to $148 at North Carolina State, $100 at Auburn, and $227 at Louisiana Tech. Cost comparisons for teachers colleges and colleges for women told the same story and prompted Chairman Marion Smith of the Board of Regents to ask if the State of Georgia could afford to do less than the average of other southeastern states?

Student Services: The second Works Report devoted an entire chapter to student personnel services in the University System. There was an urgent need to correct substandard conditions in residence halls and to adjust dormitory fees to the quality of facilities and services. Better provisions were to be made for the coordination of personnel services, health services were to be improved and extended, and the importance of diagnostic services for special student problems was to be recognized. Among the recommendations were a statewide testing program in the high schools, workshops for personnel officers, and a uniform system of student records-keeping.

Two-Year Colleges: In studying the state's junior colleges, the second Works Report turned up numerous problems. There were difficulties in reconciling two years of general education with advanced or specialized training, such as engineering, and a five-year program for junior college transfers might be the preferred solution. Chancellor Sanford, in his annual report, was convinced that at least two junior colleges should be changed into engineering schools that would prepare students to enter the senior division of Georgia Tech or any other similar technological institution.

Adult Education: The 1943 survey staff found many problems at the University System of Georgia Center. No useful educational purpose was served by offering three years of liberal arts, and resources at the center were not concentrated sufficiently on strong programs in business. The center was too dependent on part-time instructors, student fees, and excessive teaching loads for its programs and services. The center was also the only unit of the University System that was not accredited by the Southern Association of Colleges and Schools.

Physicians and Nurses: To help meet "a crying demand for physicians and nurses in Georgia," the Regents authorized in September 1944 a department of nursing at the Medical College. In a five-year nursing program, students could take their first two years at the University of Georgia, their next two years in Augusta or another approved hospital, and return to Athens for their fifth year. In a graduate nurses program, students could be given one year's academic credit for their training in a hospital school of nursing and earn a Bachelor of Science degree in nursing (or nursing education) through three additional years of work at the University of Georgia. Related to the training of physicians and nurses was the organization of public health districts, as opposed to county health departments that existed in only half of Georgia's 159 counties.

In reviewing the early years of the new University System, the accomplishments of the first decade must be regarded as commendable progress under adverse conditions. The reorganization of 26 separate and competitive state institutions and agencies into a centrally coordinated statewide system was not yet complete, but progressive steps had been taken toward educational respectability in the state's colleges and universities. The organization of the Board of Regents and the leadership of the Regents was an explicit acknowledgement of the State's responsibility for education beyond the high school and a public commitment to educational advancement.

Despite a national depression and shameful financial support, the Board of Regents was able to reduce its responsibility for secondary schoolwork by eliminating or upgrading the district A&M schools. By merging the three state institutions located in Athens, the Regents laid the foundation for a more comprehensive and viable state university. And by taking advantage of federal programs of assistance, various additions and improvements were made in the physical facilities of the University System.

Until wartime drafts and enlistments took their share of students, the total enrollment in the state's colleges had more than doubled. In 1930 no more than 6,000 students could be counted by the University of Georgia and its branches. By 1940 the total enrollment had reached 13,736 students (an increase of at least 129%). In comparison to the estimated enrollment in 1930, the enrollment of 8,035 students in 1933 makes the new University

System look even better. Less than three out of every 1,000 Georgians were students in a state-supported college, but reorganization of the University System had given better credibility to the state's efforts to provide a college education to Georgians who could afford it.

Although in great need of better financial and moral support, an organizational structure for public higher education was in place and commitments to a three-tier system of universities, senior colleges, and junior colleges were evident. Organizational problems persisted in many areas, such as the Regents' efforts to upgrade the three public colleges for blacks. Not until 1939 had the Regents been able to close the State Teachers' and Agricultural College at Forsyth and to consolidate its meager resources with the Fort Valley High and Industrial School. Even then, the establishment of Fort Valley State College was possible only with the assistance of the Rosenwald Fund. The mission and role of the public historically black institutions, as an integral part of public higher education, would not become a major item on the Regents' agenda until the 1960s.

Efforts to cope with organizational, administrative, funding, political, and social problems left many unresolved issues in educational programs and services. Significant progress had been made in attracting more competent faculty members to units of the University System but political appointees in academic positions were still detrimental to the overall improvement of higher education. Commendable steps were taken in inter-collegiate coordination by requiring survey courses and common examinations, but with continued growth, coordination would prove difficult to manage. All such problems aside, World War II brought signs of economic recovery and gave an additional boost to the University System's growth and its efforts to gain educational respectability.

In closing this discussion of the University System's first decade of progress, it is reassuring to review several observations made in the annual reports of the newly reorganized system. The 1932 Annual Report was the first of many interesting interpretations of the newly organized statewide system—and the extensive contributions of the Board of Regents, its chairman, and its appointed chancellor. No one has stated more directly the challenges of diversity than Chairman Hughes Spalding:

"Our aim is to encourage diversity of educational effort because of the diversity of human needs. . . . " (p. 20)

"During the last decade the spread of junior colleges has been very rapid, and there is no doubt but that this new institution will become a permanent part of our educational system in Georgia." (1933, p. 7)

Later chairmen would be challenged to match Chairman Spalding's diplomacy in summarizing the Board's efforts in governing 26 disparate institutions:

"This Board has worked hard and harmoniously. All important decisions have been practically unanimous. No misunderstandings nor breaches of any kind have occurred. We have avoided politics." (p. 11)

And very few annual reports would address more concisely the recurring issues of finance, tenure, local pride, and institutional aspirations:

"There is such a thing as reaching a point in finance below which we cannot, efficiently operate. . . . We have now arrived at that point." (1933, p. 14)

"At some of the institutions in the system the custom of automatically reelecting faculty members had grown up so that if a faculty member had been satisfactory for two or three years, he had a life-long job. This did not work for efficiency, and this practice was immediately discontinued." (p. 9)

"It is essential that local pride must give way to the best educational interests of the whole State. . . . It is only through this lump sum appropriation to the Regents that we will be able to preserve the integrity of such institutions as are absolutely indispensable. . . . we are asking for large powers, but they are necessary to make us equal to our task. The danger of their abuse is slight. The danger from their absence cannot be calculated." (p. 12)

CHAPTER TWO
Status and Authority: 1941-1945

> *Such matters are altogether in the control of the Board of Regents, provided the Board follows its own established rules and regulations. . . . It was the fact that we did not follow such established and agreed-upon procedures that has caused our troubles.*
>
> Chairman Sandy Beaver
> *1941 Annual Report*

The Board of Regents, with various modifications such as an increase in membership and inclusion of the governor as an *ex officio* member, operated under statutory authority from its inception in 1932 until August 3, 1943. At that time the citizens of Georgia ratified a constitutional amendment establishing the Board of Regents of the University System of Georgia as a constitutional body. Two years later the ratified amendment was incorporated into the State Constitution of 1945. The membership of the Board was increased to fifteen, one each from the ten congressional districts and five from the state at large. The governor was excluded as an *ex officio* member.

The events leading to the Board of Regents' constitutional status were the University System's severest challenge and the means by which constitutional status was granted is (a half-century later) the general public's strongest endorsement. The conditions under which several administrative officials were dismissed led to an investigation by the Southern Association of Colleges and Schools and subsequent dis-accreditation of ten University System institutions holding membership in the association. The institutions affected by the Southern Association's action were: (1) the University of Georgia, (2) Georgia School of Technology, (3) Georgia State College for Women, (4) Georgia State Woman's College, (5) Georgia Teachers' College, (6) Georgia Southwestern, (7) Middle Georgia, (8) North Georgia, (9) South Georgia, and (10) West Georgia. The three public colleges for blacks were not involved in the action because the Southern

Association did not at that time accredit the historically black institutions in its region.

In November 1941 the investigating committee held a hearing in Atlanta and invited all members of the Board of Regents and all presidents of institutions belonging to the Association. Present at the meeting were representatives of the Council on Medical Education, the American Association of Schools of Law, the American Bar Association, the American Association of Teachers Colleges, and Phi Beta Kappa Honor Society. Participants in the hearing included a committee from the Board of Regents, alumni and student committees from Georgia Tech and the University of Georgia, and the presidents of institutions affected by the recommendations of the investigating committee. Also participating were other educational officials such as the superintendent of Atlanta Public Schools (Willis A. Sutton), the president of Emory University (Goodrich C. White), and the president of Agnes Scott (J. R. McCain). Serving on the investigating committee were the presidents of Vanderbilt (O.C. Carmichael, chairman), Sewanee (Alexander Guerry), and Florida (John J. Tigert) universities.

In December 1941 the committee issued a report in which it concluded that the University System of Georgia had been the victim of "unprecedented and unjustifiable political interference." The Governor of Georgia had violated not only "sound educational policy, but proper democratic procedure in insisting upon the resignation of members of the Board of Regents to appoint to that body men who would do his bidding." The Board of Regents had violated sound educational procedure "in dismissals and appointment of staff members." The committee further concluded that "every institution in the System is affected by the precedents established and by the actions already taken." Where such conditions exist, the committee stated, "there can be no effective educational program."

The specific findings of the committee were particularly detrimental to the purposes and functions of the University System. Finding that Governor Eugene Talmadge had first requested that the Board of Regents dismiss Dr. Walter D. Cocking, dean of education at the University of Georgia, and then denounced the Regents' action when they failed to do so, the committee detailed the governor's subsequent actions in: (1) forcing the resignation of three members of the Board, (2) appointing three members who would do his bidding, (3) notifying Dean Cocking that he would be tried again, and (4) summoning President Marvin Pittman of Georgia Teachers' College for trial on the same date.

From the record the committee noted that Dean Cocking and President Pittman were dismissed "by the same vote" and with the same "mockery of democratic procedure." The committee was convinced by its examination of the evidence that the charges against the two were "either spurious or entirely unsupported by the evidence."

The committee also found that in addition to Dean Cocking and President Pittman, the Board of Regents had dismissed—without hearings, adequate reasons, or due notice—Dr. J. Curtis Dixon, vice chancellor of the University System; Dr. Chester M. Destler, chairman of the Division of Social Science at Georgia Teachers' College; the dean of women and another faculty member at Georgia Teachers' College; one faculty member at North Georgia College; and three staff members of the Department of Agricultural Extension.

In a related matter the committee found that the position of dean of men had been filled at the Georgia School of Technology without the recommendation of either President Brittain or Chancellor Sanford. The committee recognized that the appointee did not accept the position but that fact did not alter the conviction of the committee that the Board of Regents had violated sound educational policy in the appointment. The committee also recognized that the governor under the statutes of the state had the authority to modify the University System's budget in any way he saw fit. He had the authority to delete or modify any item of expenditure or remove any individual from the payroll without the Board's approval. To the committee, however, "arbitrary power of this kind in the hands of any individual or agency is a threat to sound procedure in the operation of an educational system."

The committee made but two recommendations: (1) that the ten (named) institutions be dropped from membership in the Southern Association of Colleges and Schools, and (2) that the suspension take effect September 1, 1942 and continue until removed by vote at the association's next (or later) annual meeting. The committee's recommendations were judicious in not taking immediate effect and challenging in view of the forthcoming gubernatorial election to be held in the fall of 1942. The date of the committee's report was December 3rd, just four days prior to the United States entry into the Second World War.

The decisiveness of the 1942 gubernatorial election was further testimony to the damaging effects of political interference. The incumbent governor was defeated by a candidate committed to the University System's re-accreditation. The successful candidate received 58 percent of the popular vote and 64 percent of the county unit vote that were then required in Georgia primaries. Upon taking office on January 12, 1943 Governor Ellis Arnall (1943-1947) gained legislative cooperation in submitting a constitutional amendment that would grant constitutional authority to the Board of Regents. The House and Senate bills for the constitutional amendment were passed without a dissenting vote within eleven days of the new governor's oath of office. Upon passage of the House and Senate bills, the governor (by executive order) appointed a new Board of Regents, reinstating several members who had resigned under partisan political pressure. The constitutional amendment was ratified by Georgia voters on August 3, 1943 and became a section in the Constitution of 1877. Although the issue was convincingly resolved by the Georgia electorate, the process had taken more than two years and the total cost in public and human resources was incalculable.

The Constitution of 1945

In March 1943 the General Assembly passed a resolution providing for a commission to revise the state's constitution. The commission, consisting of 26 members and led by Governor Arnall, submitted its revision to the General Assembly in January 1945, and on August 7, 1945 the new constitution was approved by the voters of the state. Over 90 percent of its provisions were drawn from the amended Constitution of 1877.

The constitutional authority of the Board of Regents was unaltered. Article VIII, Section IV provided for "the government, control, and management" of the University System and "all of its institutions" by a fifteen-member board that was representative of the ten congressional districts and the state at large. Appointments to the Board were for terms of seven years each, a stipulation related to the governor's four-year term of office. At that time the governor could succeed himself, and the staggered seven-year appointments of Regents would thereby prevent a single governor from appointing all members of the Board. In the event of vacancies caused by resignation, death, or from causes other than the expiration of term, the Board of Regents was authorized (in a provision later altered) to elect a successor who would hold office until the end of the next session of the General Assembly.

Strongly implied in the conditions of appointment were the independence of the Board of Regents as a governing body, and its freedom from political interference by the governor and the state legislature. Also implicit was the Regents' authority and independence in electing a chancellor who would recommend institutional presidents to the Board. In turn, institutional presidents would recommend to the chancellor the faculty and staff appointments for their particular units. Directly related to powers of appointment were the Regents' authority and responsibility in all matters pertaining to the dismissal of faculty members.

In brief, the new constitution gave the Board of Regents broad governing powers for its own procedures, the internal operations of the chancellor's staff, and the administration, management, and/or control of the respective units of the University System. Not only was the Board responsible for systemwide policies, the Board was responsible for institutional policies affecting daily operations on the various campuses. The gist of the Regents' constitutional status was their authority and responsibility as a state-level governing board for all public institutions of higher education regarded as units of the University System of Georgia.

Powers and Policies of the Regents

The Board of Regents executes its constitutional responsibilities in two primary ways: (a) by adopting policies to provide general guidelines for governing the University System, and (b) by electing the chancellor of the System and, upon his recommendation, presidents of the institutions who are given the responsibility and the authority for the administration of the System in accord with the adopted policies (*Policy Manual, Board of Regents [2nd ed.], 1982*). In the execution of its responsibilities, the Board of Regents has the power to make "such reasonable rules and regulations as are necessary for the performance of its duties." The Regents' powers of appointment cover "professors, educators, stewards, or any other officers necessary for all of the schools in the University System," the discontinuance of their services when required for "the good of the System or any of its schools or institutions," and the determination of their salaries and/or compensations. All such actions are taken in accordance with state law and must not be in conflict with the state constitution or the authority granted other constitutional agencies.

In implementing their broad powers as a statewide governing board, the Regents have been primarily concerned with institutions, programs, and personnel. In the early years of their new powers the Regents were responsible for six senior institutions, seven junior colleges, three colleges for blacks, and three experiment stations. Also included among the Regents' governing responsibilities was the Department of Adult Education with its two divisions, the Georgia Evening College and the Division of General Extension in Atlanta. The officers of the first constitutional Board were Chairman Marion Smith, Vice Chairman Sandy Beaver, Chancellor S. V. Sanford, Secretary L. R. Siebert, and Treasurer W. Wilson Noyes. The standing committees on which members of the Board served were the committees on education, finance, organization and law, agriculture, and visitation.

The Board's concern with programs at that time was directed to the postwar years, the enrichment or modification of coursework for returning servicemen, and efforts to strengthen the state's teacher education programs. New curricula were necessary in the postwar era to accommodate changes in "the concept of the place of women in society" and to prepare students for occupations in the fields of management and health care. In later years the committee structure of the Board and the chancellor's staff changed with demands for new institutions and with the many changes in personnel and public expectations.

Members of the Board

Neither state law nor Regents policies specify qualifications for individual members of the Board. Each Regent need only be appointed by the governor and confirmed by the Senate. Public expectations are explicit, however, and members of the Board serve in the public interest and not at the pleasure of the governor. In the public's estimation, appointment to the Board of Regents is the highest honor that the State of Georgia can confer upon nonelected officials.

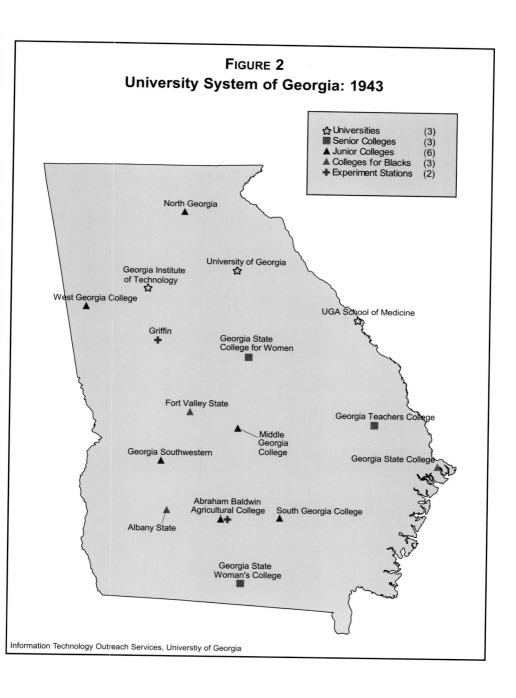

FIGURE 2
University System of Georgia: 1943

☆ Universities (3)
■ Senior Colleges (3)
▲ Junior Colleges (6)
▲ Colleges for Blacks (3)
✚ Experiment Stations (2)

North Georgia ▲

University of Georgia ☆

Georgia Institute of Technology ☆

West Georgia College ▲

UGA School of Medicine ☆

Griffin ✚

Georgia State College for Women ■

Fort Valley State ▲

Georgia Teachers College ■

Middle Georgia College ▲

Georgia Southwestern ▲

Georgia State College ▲

Abraham Baldwin Agricultural College ▲✚

South Georgia College ▲

Albany State ▲

Georgia State Woman's College ■

Information Technology Outreach Services, Universtiy of Georgia

Since the Board's creation one hundred and thirty-nine citizens of Georgia have served as members. At least twenty-seven Regents have been re-appointed for one or more terms and one Regent (Carey Williams) served for thirty years. Almost without exception, the individual Regents have been leaders in agriculture, business, finance, real estate, and the professions of law or medicine. Until the 1970s most Regents had been male, white, financially secure, college-educated, and Protestant. Many have been graduates of the institutions for which they were constitutionally responsible.

In keeping with other members of governing boards, Regents regard their major responsibilities as the review and approval of institutional policy decisions, the appointment of presidents, and the approval of other decisions related to faculties and students. As members of a statewide governing board, Regents are also responsible for the allocation (among institutions) of public funds and resources. Members of the Board of Regents may also serve as trustees of private or independent colleges *(Best, 1988)*.

Officers of the Board

The administrative structure and activities of the central offices have changed as the Board of Regents and University System institutions have acquired new functions and responsibilities. The duties and responsibilities of the officers were later defined in the following manner:

The *Chairman* presides at meetings of the Board with the authority to vote, appoints members of all committees, and designates the chairman of each committee. He or she is an *ex officio* member of all committees with the authority to vote. Upon the authority of the Board (and in the name of Board of Regents) the chairman executes all notes, bonds, deeds, contracts, and other documents requiring the seal of the Board of Regents of the University System of Georgia. The chairman also submits the annual report of the Board of Regents to the governor *(Bylaws, Article IV, Section 5)*. The power and influence of the chairman has varied over the years and with the capabilities of individuals serving in the position. In the early years of the University System the chairman served somewhat as a chief executive officer while the chancellor served primarily as a chief of staff. This arrangement was no longer necessary when Phillip Weltner, a member of the Board, became chancellor. Later chairmen of the Board have provided leadership as the strengths and weaknesses of chancellors required.

The *Vice Chairman* performs the duties and has the powers of the chairman during the latter's absence or disability (*Bylaws, Article IV, Section 6*). As the chairmanship became a rotating position in the 1980s, vice chairmen were elected with expectations of being the next chairman.

The *Chancellor* is elected by the Regents and holds office at the pleasure of the Board. In the event of a vacancy in the chancellorship, the Board names an acting chancellor who serves until the office of the chancellor is filled. The chancellor is now clearly identified as the chief administrative officer of the University System *and* the chief executive officer of the Board of Regents. He is responsible to the Board for the prompt and effective execution of all resolutions, policies, rules, and regulations adopted by the Board for the operation of the entire University System and for the government of any and all of its institutions. With such responsibilities comes broad discretionary powers that enable him to perform all duties prescribed by the Board (*BR Minutes, 1980-81, p. 241*). Since 1932 eight individuals have served as chancellor with two others serving as acting chancellor (without later appointment as chancellor). The nature of the leadership provided by each has necessarily varied with the individual's understanding of his responsibilities and the different challenges to which the chief administrative officer of a statewide university system must respond.

The *Executive Vice Chancellor* is elected by the Board upon recommendation of the chancellor. The executive vice chancellor acts as the chancellor's deputy and speaks for the chancellor (in his absence). All members of the chancellor's staff report to the executive vice chancellor who is responsible for organizing the work of the staff and for its oversight. The executive vice chancellor also reviews all appointments and budget amendments in the University System. He arranges for the preparation of budgets, building programs, and the agenda for meetings of the Board of Regents. As the chancellor's deputy the executive vice chancellor also conducts day-to-day institutional operations that do not interfere with the presidents' direct and immediate access to the chancellor (*BR Minutes, 1970-71, pp. 24-25*).

The *Executive Secretary* is also elected by the Board upon the recommendation of the chancellor. He is required to be present at all meetings of the Board and at committee meetings except as otherwise determined by the Board. He keeps an accurate record of the proceedings of the meetings of the Board and of committees and is responsible for maintaining the Policy Manual. He receives and processes all applications for reviews and other appeals submitted to the Board. In addition, the executive secretary keeps in safe custody the seal of the Board and affixes the seal to those documents requiring it. He is the custodian of all deeds and evidence of title to the tangible property of the University System, acts as general counsel for the Board, advises and consults with the chancellor and the several institutions on all legal matters, and serves as the principal liaison between the Board and the Attorney General's office (*Bylaws, Article IV, Section 8*).

The *Treasurer* is another officer of the Board elected by the Board upon the recommendation of the chancellor. He is present at all meetings of the Board except as otherwise determined by the Board. In the performance of his duties he is placed under bond in an amount determined by the Board (*BR Minutes, 1980-81, p. 241*).

The Chancellor's Staff

As the chancellor's duties and responsibilities have expanded with the growth of the University System, his staff was enlarged accordingly. The position of assistant chancellor was used in the 1950s and a director of plant operations was added to the chancellor's staff in the 1960s. The title of vice chancellor was not used until 1964 when Dr. S. Walter Martin became vice chancellor for academic affairs prior to becoming acting chancellor. In 1966 Dr. Fred C. Davison became vice chancellor and Dr. Mario J. Goglia became vice chancellor—research. Two new vice chancellors were added the following year when a vice chancellor—services was appointed and the position of treasurer became that of vice chancellor—fiscal affairs and treasurer. In such ways positions on the chancellor's staff were given functional titles and a functional division of staff responsibilities has continued since that time. The position of vice chancellor is now used for the administrative functions of student services, research and planning, and information technology. Positions of assistant vice chancellor

are used in the areas of academic affairs, affirmative action, facilities, fiscal affairs, planning, and research while an assistant-to-the-
chancellor title is used in public relations and information services.

Procedural Policies

The Board of Regents, under its bylaws, meets monthly on
the second Wednesday. Special meetings may be called by the
chairman upon written request to the executive secretary, or by
the executive secretary upon written requests from four or more
members of the Board. All meetings are held in the board room
of the Regents unless otherwise determined by the Board. Meetings begin at 10:00 a.m. with eight members of the Board con-
stituting a quorum. Parliamentary rules of the state Senate are
followed in conducting the business of the Board.

Standing committees of the Board are: (1) Executive Committee, consisting of the chairman, the immediate past chairman, the
vice chairman, and the chancellor *ex officio* nonvoting; (2) Committee on Buildings and Grounds; (3) Committee on Desegregation;
(4) Committee on Education; (5) Committee on Finance and
Business; (6) Committee on Health Professions; (7) Committee
on Organization and Law; (8) Committee on Research and Extension; and (9) Committee on Visitation. Each standing committee
consists of not less than three, nor more than five members
(Policy Manual, 1982).

Academic and administrative policies for the institutions of
the University System are developed through an advisory council
of institutional presidents and two nonvoting members from each
institution who are selected by their respective presidents. Under
the advisory council are various academic committees, representing the programs of instruction within each of the units, and
various administrative committees, addressing such matters as
personnel, student financial aid, and general extension. The academic and administrative committees make recommendations
to the advisory council which, in turn, makes recommendations
to the chancellor.

The Constitution of 1982

In 1982 a new state constitution was adopted in which two
slight modifications were made in the Board of Regents' authority. The Regents themselves can no longer appoint a temporary

successor in the event of a vacancy on the Board; that privilege was reserved for the governor. Another slight difference between the 1982 Constitution and the 1945 Constitution pertains to "approval by majority vote in the House of Representatives and the Senate" of new public colleges, junior colleges, and universities created in the Board's exercise of its "exclusive authority" to create such institutions. Approval by the General Assembly was *not* required in Board decisions to change the status of any institution existing prior to the 1982 Constitution.

The Constitution of 1982, as shown in Appendix A, sustains and enhances the Board of Regents authority and responsibility for the state's comprehensive system of public higher education. As a constitutional board, the Regents have extensive powers for the governance and administration of 34 public institutions and for the implementation of public and institutional policy. In all matters dealing with state and federal government, the Regents serve as the representatives of public higher education within the state. In the coalescence of its governing authority under a single constitutional board, the Regents also serve as a safeguard against political interference and/or undue public or private intervention. In meeting their responsibilities the Regents also serve as a public advocate of higher education as essential to the State's social, economic, technological, and cultural advancement.

Careful review would show that the Board of Regents uses its authority sparingly. Commendable restraint is evident in the setting of both system and institutional policies. The purposes of the System itself have always been stated in general terms with a minimum of educational doctrine. Institutions have been defined mostly by level and major functions instead of specific missions or roles. Programs have been classified in broad terms that suggest areas of teaching and learning and not in terms of state needs and public expectations.

The administrative structure and functions of the central offices were, and would continue to be, a matter of cut-and-try. As different individuals were appointed to administrative positions, duties and responsibilities were defined to fit personal qualifications and position requirements. When the demands of the position were incompatible with the capabilities of the person, the position was reorganized or abolished in search of a more suitable fit. The chancellor's position as chief academic officer of the institutions and as chief executive officer for the Board, along with the positions of executive secretary and treasurer, have been the constants in central administration. Other administrative and staff functions have varied appreciably with the times and the conditions imposed.

The authority and responsibility of the chancellor are crucial to the effective administration and governance of the University System—just as the authority and responsibility of presidents are essential to institutional leadership. No other appointed or elected public official demonstrates more clearly the state's need for educational leadership or serves so well as a spokesman for public policy in higher education. And with the possible exception of the governor, no other public official experiences the public respect shown the University System chancellor.

If two guiding principles may be identified for the policy decisions of the Board (and the state's purpose in providing public resources), one can be called self-sufficiency and the other geographical accessibility. The first principle was evident in the early years as Georgians accepted responsibility for their own education and lessened their dependence on other states and institutions for educated, professionally prepared participants in the state's economic and cultural life. The second principle became increasingly evident in the postwar years when higher education became the focal point of "rising expectations." Geographical accessibility was evident in the location of institutions inherited by the Regents and geographical distribution became a dominant factor in the establishment of later institutions.

CHAPTER THREE
Expansion and Improvement: 1946-1960

> In spending money for the expansion and improvement
> of the institutions of the System, it is essential that the
> expenditures be made for the attainment of clearly defined
> institutional objectives and that they be made in accordance
> with a well formulated, long-range plan of development.
>
> Chancellor Harmon W. Caldwell
> 1951 Annual Report

The first fourteen years (1932-1946) of the University System are appreciated best as years in which the Regents reorganized the state's institutions of public higher education and established their authority as a statewide governing board. No institution, however, deserved status as a full-fledged university despite surveys by outside educators. The University System was not yet a statewide system of colleges and universities serving the educational needs of Georgia residents, and Georgians, like other southerners, were dependent upon other states for much of their scientific, professional, and technical expertise. Thus, 1946-1960 can be viewed as years of postwar growth and expansion, and as years in which progress was more rapid and more substantive.

The Strayer Report

In 1949 the Board of Regents again found funds for a statewide survey by out-of-state experts and specialists. The survey began in September of that year and was concluded on December 15th in time for consideration and action by the General Assembly convening in January 1950. The director of the survey was George D. Strayer, formerly director of the Division of Field Studies at Teachers College, Columbia University. Although submitted as "a staff report," the published report has always been known as the "Strayer Report." Like its predecessors, the Works reports, the Strayer Report was simply entitled "A Report of a Survey of the University System of Georgia."

More extensive in scope and more intensive in its analyses than the Works reports, the Strayer Report was a comprehensive study of the University System of Georgia in the years following World War II and the closest thing to a plan for systemwide development the Regents had until the Governor's (Carl Sanders) Commission To Improve Education in the 1960s. The Strayer Report addressed each of the issues identified in the second Works Report and arrived at many recommendations that were compatible with the earlier surveys but made some recommendations that were contrary.

The Strayer Report began by meeting head-on one of the University System's most irritating problems. The first lines in the report read, "The competitive ambitions of individual institutions must be subordinated to the responsibilities of the state-wide system of higher education" *(p. 1)*. The report then restated the Regents' responsibilities, their delegation of specific activities and functions to the separate institutions, and their maintenance of authority through "supervisory officers." To Strayer, the most important contribution that any institution could make to the social and economic development of the state was the preparation of professional personnel for service in the state's colleges and schools. Explicit recognition was given the University System's responsibility to prepare college and university teachers and administrators.

The report stressed that to prepare professionally trained teachers for the public schools, the University System should recognize a minimum standard of four years of college training and move from there to higher standards. Facilities were to be improved and increased for such purposes, with "a broad general education" as "a necessary portion of any program" *(p. 11)*. Evidently to settle territorial squabbles, the survey staff recommended the form and level of programs that each institution should develop. Georgia Tech and the state's junior colleges were to enter no field of teacher education while the University of Georgia was to be the state's one comprehensive teacher preparatory institution. The "special fields" of education (agriculture, home economics, physical education, business education, fine and industrial arts) were "allocated" to the other institutions on the basis of faculties and facilities. Academic subjects (English, science, history, mathematics, etc.) were not similarly allocated but assumed to be a function of four-year colleges preparing high school teachers for specific fields.

In addition to laboratory schools for practice teaching, the University System needed programs for the inservice training of teachers already employed in the public schools. A need that could not "be too strongly emphasized" was in the areas of research, graduate work, and professional education. The University System's paucity of resources in these areas was charitably treated by the survey staff, but the discouraging state of public higher education was nonetheless evident. Recommended as "the one great center for graduate and professional education and for research" was the University of Georgia. The Georgia Institute of Technology was to be permitted to add a doctoral degree in mathematics to Ph.D.'s already authorized in physics and chemistry while the Medical College was to remain an independent unit and offer the master's degree in the clinical and technological fields of medicine.

Noting that in March 1949 the Regents had at last merged the Agricultural Experiment Stations and the Cooperative Extension Service with the UGA College of Agriculture, the survey staff endorsed the Regents' authority in matters of internal organization for the College of Agriculture and recommended the establishment of an agricultural research council. They then suggested that the organization and procedures of agricultural research might serve as a pattern for other organized research units within the University System.

The Strayer Report strongly emphasized the linkage of research with graduate education and endorsed the organization of graduate schools with a right to designate graduate faculty members who were qualified for graduate instruction. Such a school was also given the right to approve any course to be taken for graduate credit and have its own budgeted funds to encourage research and thereby tie research more firmly to graduate instruction.

In considering the diverse extension services offered within the University System, the survey staff concluded that an "institutional division" of extension services along geographical or functional lines was impractical and recommended the "voluntary or compulsory coordination" of extension services to form one statewide agency. Coordination was to be a responsibility of a system officer on the chancellor's staff who would be assisted by an Extension Council representative of the various institutions. The general extension service of the University of Georgia had many elements which the survey staff believed applicable to the statewide effort.

Institutional Functions: The mission or role of each unit of the University System was well defined in the Strayer Report. Georgia Tech, the Medical College, North Georgia, Georgia State College for Women, and Georgia Teachers' College were assigned distinctive missions in keeping with their titles and their historical development. Valdosta State was to be developed as a co-educational college of arts and sciences, with a program for preparing elementary school teachers. The University of Georgia was to continue as the major institution in the University System with a full range of undergraduate, graduate, and professional programs and with broad applications of its research and extension services.

The delineation of roles for the historically black institutions was quite explicit. Fort Valley State was to be the State's college for emphasizing agriculture and home economics, with possibilities for granting master's degrees in those fields. Savannah State was to be developed in industrial and business fields, with secondary emphases on elementary teacher education and programs in the arts and sciences. Albany State was to be the state's college of arts and sciences, with a larger emphasis on elementary teacher education than the other two historically black institutions.

The difficult unit for the survey staff was the Atlanta Division of the University of Georgia. Although recommending independent status for the institution, the survey staff confined their recommendation to the awarding of bachelor's degrees in business administration. Only two years of academic work were to be given in arts and sciences but "pending the establishment of a junior college by the City of Atlanta," the institution was to continue offering two-year diploma programs in business. These recommendations were implemented six years later when the Atlanta Division became the Georgia State College of Business Administration.

In a separate chapter the Strayer Report fully delineated the role and functions of the state's junior colleges but recommended their disassociation from the University System. The junior college "movement" was depicted as the addition of upper division work to a state's common school system. Providing two-year vocational programs for students uninterested in a collegiate education, junior colleges nonetheless offered general education as a strong component of terminal or career curricula and served also to prepare students for transfer to four-year colleges, if they so desired. As "a local institution" a junior college also provided a program of adult education. Thus, they were to be administered by local school boards, or by another board representative of a larger area that was to constitute a junior college district. Junior colleges would be, of course, under the general supervision of the State Board of Education and the State was to continue to support them, along with funds raised through local taxation. Although eloquent in persuasion and fifteen pages in length, this particular chapter contained not one single recommendation ever implemented by the Board of Regents.

Postwar Adjustments: The Strayer Report was a milestone in the University System's development for many reasons. It depicted in great detail the status of public higher education in the years following World War II and demonstrated the changes in institutional composition that had taken place since the University System's creation seventeen years earlier. When the Strayer Report was received by the Regents, they were responsible for fifteen institutions of higher education, an appreciable reduction from the twenty-six units they had inherited. If the Evening School and Technical Institute of Georgia Tech were counted separately, the total number was seventeen. Three of these units remained colleges for blacks; five were two-year or junior colleges; and at least seven were senior institutions.

Only indirectly did the Strayer Report reveal the implementation or ignorance of recommendations found in the earlier Works reports. Middle Georgia and South Georgia colleges were still intact; North Georgia was a four-year college; and the Atlanta Division was accredited only by virtue of its designation as a division of the University of Georgia. Per-student instructional costs were still lower at the Atlanta Division ($195) than anywhere else and student fees still accounted for the majority of institutional income. Georgians still paid a higher proportion (34.2%) of their educational costs than other southerners (21.8%) or Americans (18.6%) did. And yet, the University System had grown significantly and was, by most measures, a stronger, more mature system of public higher education. Not unrelated to its growth and development was its weathering of disaccreditation by the Southern Association of Colleges and Schools in the early 1940s because of political interference and its later inclusion as a constitutional body in the new state Constitution adopted in 1945.

The Strayer Report may be read, nonetheless, as an indictment of educational quality following the unplanned growth of the postwar years. Returning veterans overcrowded classrooms as they took advantage of the G.I. Bill. Student housing, food services, and student personnel programs could only be judged as deplorable for most campuses. Dormitory facilities and services were frequently inadequate because of "deferred maintenance" during the war and their excessive use in the years immediately following. Overcrowding created, in many cases, what the survey staff regarded as "a serious health hazard" and the obsolescence of some buildings was "a grave menace" to student safety.

To solve its "deferred maintenance problems" the University System would need, according to survey staff estimates, almost $1.4 million—over $600,000 at Georgia Tech alone. With almost no exceptions, dormitories on the separate campuses were operated at an appreciable profit. Seldom had the need for planning been more clearly demonstrated.

Financing the Future: The Strayer Report gave close attention to the administration and governance of the University System; its budgeting, accounting, and reporting needs; and its organizational structure and procedures. The report then addressed the University System's need for adequate financing in its efforts to meet increased demands for education beyond the high school. Enrollments in the University System were shown as almost doubling (81.4%) in the decade of the 1940s and projected enrollments were given up to 1964-1965. Veterans were expected to have received all educational benefits by the mid 1950s, but the projected enrollments were necessarily low because of educational trends and developments that the survey staff could not take into consideration. The estimated demand for the services of the University System showed a decline until 1954-1955 and a slow, gradual increase until 1964-1965 when enrollments were expected to exceed 44,000 students.

In retrospect, the recommendations of the Strayer Report were understandably cautious. Faculty salaries were to be raised an average of 12.5 percent; at least $250,000 was needed for various improvements within the system and the strengthening of graduate education; and the Atlanta Division was to receive another $250,000 for needed improvements there. The sum of $80,000 would permit the Regents to add needed specialists to their central office staff.

To meet its financial needs, the University System should seek support from the state on the basis of "comprehensive plans looking to the future." Aid from philanthropy was also to be sought but not to the extent that it might reduce state support. Tuition was to be reduced to about 25 percent so that students paid a smaller proportion of their educational expenses. Housing, food, and other student services were to be improved but offered to students at a figure much closer to actual cost. And finally, if state support for current operations and capital outlay could be increased immediately to $13.2 million (an absolute increase of $7.7 million), the annual appropriation at this level should suffice until about 1958.

Postwar Growth

If the years 1946-1960 are regarded as the University System's second phase of development, they can be interpreted as a period in which the Board of Regents was actively concerned with the System's growth and expansion, campus planning and development, adequate funding, and the internal improvement of institutional programs and services. Policy making was not highly centralized, however, and most policy decisions were made on an *ad hoc* basis or in a piecemeal manner. Many decisions were based on informal studies and the recommendations of particular councils or committees who dealt with specific issues and problems.

In the early 1950s the Board of Regents was obviously concerned with the implementation of the major recommendations of the Strayer Report. The Georgia State Woman's College in Valdosta opened its doors to males and its title was changed to Valdosta State College. The University of Georgia School of Medicine became the Medical College of Georgia and was authorized to offer the master's degree in selected fields. The re-organization of agricultural programs in instruction, research, and cooperative extension was completed, and the functions of the State's three colleges for blacks were re-defined. Albany State College was designated as the state's liberal arts college for blacks, and the curricula at Albany State and Savannah State were altered to conform to the re-defined missions of the three institutions.

The size and status of the University System in 1950 are indicated by its 1,095 faculty members, a cumulative enrollment of 29,011 students, and 5,309 awarded degrees. The University of Georgia did not confer a Ph.D. in 1950 but Georgia Tech conferred *one*, along with 108 masters. The Atlanta Division of the University of Georgia conferred 72 Bachelor of Business Administration degrees and 242 Bachelors of Commercial Science. WWII veterans, taking advantage of the GI Bill, constituted 40 percent of the cumulative enrollment in 1949-1950.

During the next academic year the impact of the declining enrollment of veterans was severely felt when the cumulative enrollment declined 14.3 percent and a special allocation of $92,000 was necessary to cover the deficits resulting from departing veterans. For 1951-1952, however, state appropriations were raised to $12.3 million, more than twice the amount received in previous years. In implementing the recommendations of the Strayer Report, the borrowing limit of the University System Building Authority was increased from $12 million to $20 million, thereby enabling the Board of Regents to continue its building program. Long-range development studies were initiated during 1950-1951 and completed for nine institutions.

The number of University System faculty members declined in the early 1950s, but significant increases were observed in faculty members holding the Ph.D. and a significant reduction in the number of those holding only a bachelor's degree. In 1951-1952 the University of Georgia conferred three Ph.D.'s while Georgia Tech conferred two. Cumulative enrollments within the System were down 17.7 percent and the enrollment of veterans declined from 7,204 the previous year to 3,792 in FY52. The decline of *non-veteran* students was attributed, in part, to the addition of a twelfth grade by many Georgia high schools. When the number fell to 999 FTE faculty members in FY52, the Board of Regents took steps to strengthen faculties by annual salaries that were 20 percent higher and by the adoption of uniform policies for: (a) appointment and promotion, (b) tenure, and (c) compulsory retirement at the age of 67 instead of 70 as in previous years.

Student enrollments continued to decline until 1954 when the beginning of an upward trend was noted by the chancellor

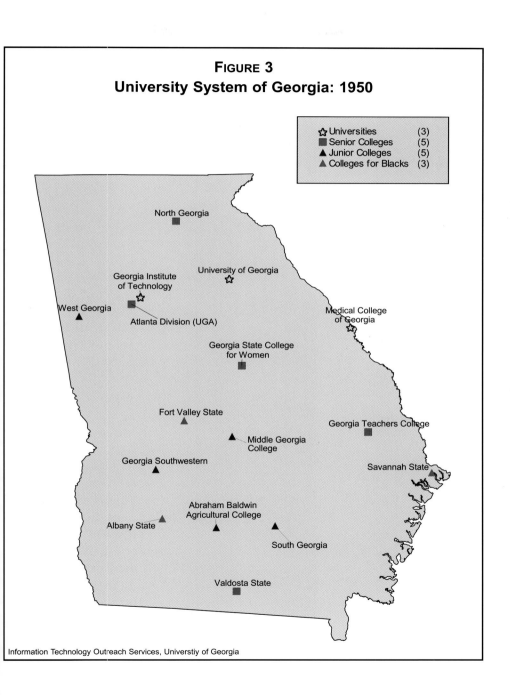

FIGURE 3
University System of Georgia: 1950

☆ Universities (3)
■ Senior Colleges (5)
▲ Junior Colleges (5)
▲ Colleges for Blacks (3)

North Georgia

Georgia Institute of Technology

University of Georgia

West Georgia

Atlanta Division (UGA)

Medical College of Georgia

Georgia State College for Women

Fort Valley State

Georgia Teachers College

Middle Georgia College

Georgia Southwestern

Savannah State

Abraham Baldwin Agricultural College

Albany State

South Georgia

Valdosta State

Information Technology Outreach Services, Universtiy of Georgia

in his annual report. New degree programs were authorized at the doctoral level, research programs were improved, and significant changes in undergraduate programs were made.

External Review and Study

In 1955 the House of Representatives appointed a sub-committee to study the operations and needs of the University System. Members of the sub-committee were: J. Ebb Duncan, chairman; Mac Barber; Braswell Deen, Jr.; W. C. Massee; and Jack Murr. This study committee visited all units of the University System, interviewed campus officials, and prepared a report setting forth the conditions and needs of the various units. The committee recommended an annual appropriation of $23.7 million.

During 1955 the University System's inadequate financial support received extensive publicity in the Atlanta newspapers and a special session of the General Assembly was called for the purpose of raising additional revenue. The additional funds allocated to the Board of Regents in FY56 were $3.1 million.

Related to the state's increased support of higher education were the separation (September 1, 1955) of the Atlanta Division from the University of Georgia and the change of its title to the Georgia State College of Business Administration. Changes in institutional status had been recommended in the second Works Report and the Strayer Report but needed the spur of new accreditation requirements adopted in 1954 by the Southern Association of College and Schools.

Other Significant Policy Decisions

The conversion of the Atlanta Division to Georgia State College was the first major change in institutional status during the 1950s. The Board of Regents moved (in 1956) their central offices from Georgia State to 244 Washington Street. Dr. Joseph E. Moore of Georgia Tech was temporarily appointed director of testing and guidance for the University System in 1956 and conducted a systemwide study of testing and guidance needs in public higher education. At its September 1956 meeting the Board adopted the College Board Scholastic Aptitude Test (SAT) as an admission requirement to units of the University System. Uses of the test by institutional officials were expected to "profoundly influence the institution's instructional program" (1956 *Annual Report*).

The National Defense Education Act of 1958 rekindled national interest in testing and counseling as it addressed the most pressing educational issues of identifying and training scientific, technical, and professional manpower. The Georgia Nuclear Advisory Commission, appointed by Governor Ernest Vandiver to study the impact of nuclear energy on the state's economic development, created four task forces to study: (a) testing, counseling, and guidance; (b) teacher education; (c) vocational education; and (d) educational television. Each task force prepared and published a report making recommendations to the Committee on Manpower and Education, chaired by William M. Suttles, dean of students at Georgia State. The staff director of these studies was Dr. Doak Campbell, president emeritus of Florida State University.

The reports on vocational and teacher education stressed the need for more extensive, improved programs that would meet the changing demands and expectations of society, but the report on educational television received the most attention from the public. Educational television was a far more appealing topic to the public and one that offered considerable promise for the future of education.

The task force on testing, counseling, and guidance was representative of the state's institutions of higher education, business and financial firms, and the State Health Department. The published report of the task force pointed to an expected college enrollment of 72,000 students in 1965, an increase of 71 percent over the recorded enrollment of students in 1955. To provide testing, counseling, and guidance for over 40,000 college students there were fewer than 30 professionally trained faculty or staff members in the entire state. An important recommendation, therefore, asked for a study of present facilities and programs for training counselors, one of the major provisions of the National Defense Education Act. Education and training programs should contain adequate coursework in testing and statistics as part of a minimum core for all teachers. Anticipated by this particular task force was an increased use in educational achievement tests, as well as aptitude tests, for college admissions. At least four institutions in 1959 already required College Board achievement tests, as well as the SAT. Also anticipated was widespread use of "high-speed electronic computers" for admission and placement decisions.

Regents Office of Testing and Guidance

From its organization in 1957 to its demise in the late 1960s, the Regents Office of Testing and Guidance, under the direction of Dr. John R. Hills, provided a wealth of information to admission officers, counselors, and others concerned with the prediction of academic performance in units of the University System. An annual norms booklet was prepared in which SAT scores, high school grades, and college grades were analyzed for each of the institutions admitting students at the freshman level. By differentially weighting SAT-Verbal scores, SAT-Mathematics scores, and high school averages for its previous freshman class, prediction equations were developed for each institution. Included in each norms booklet was technical advice on the uses of predicted freshman grades for college admissions. Other publications of the Office provided assistance to high school counselors in their efforts to help individual students (*Counselor's Guide*, 1959).

An unusually informative feature of each norms booklet was the distributions, with means and standard deviations, of SAT scores and high school averages for all freshmen entering University System institutions. In the fall of 1958, for example, the average SAT-Verbal and SAT-Mathematics scores for 6,081 freshmen were 396 and 433, respectively. In high school these students had earned grades averaging 2.7 (on a 4.0 scale). In their freshman coursework they had earned slightly lower grade-point-averages, depending on the institution and the field of study. One of the additional benefits of the annual norms booklets was the encouragement given to more uniform grading practices in both high schools and colleges.

By 1960 the annual norms booklet had become a valuable source of information on the abilities and achievement of students entering the University System. Enrollment had increased to 7,297 students, and SAT scores with high school grades gave an excellent overview of student preparation for academic coursework at the college level. The mean high school average reported for freshmen was a "B" and the mean SAT scores of 427 on the verbal scale and 466 on the mathematics scale indicated substantial competencies in dealing with verbal and numerical concepts. A noticeable number of the entering freshmen scored below 400 on the verbal and mathematical scales, however, and only a relatively few scored above 600 on the two scales. In brief, no more than 5 percent of the entering freshmen displayed exceptional promise for academic coursework and roughly one-half of the group had verbal and mathematical abilities that suggested disadvantages in advanced or specialized work at the junior and senior levels. At least 10 percent of the 1960 entering freshmen had gained entrance to a unit of the University System with less than a "C" average.

The productivity of the staff is evidenced in other ways by the numerous journal articles and research bulletins published in the early 1960s. As other institutions in other states resorted to selective admissions as a means of coping with increased enrollments, the Regents' program became a model of statewide testing that received national attention. In addition to their research, the professional staff was quite active in workshops and conferences conducted for admission officers, counselors, and other student personnel workers. In each of these efforts there was innovation and leadership in developing a systemwide testing program and a statewide concern with student advisement, guidance, and counseling.

Selective Admissions

As college applications increased in the late 1950s, many colleges adopted higher admission standards as a means of controlling course enrollments and the increasing demands placed on college faculties and facilities. In particular, institutions with limited facilities and little room for expansion turned to selective admissions as a way of maintaining traditional images and missions. Institutions with unfilled classrooms and dormitories responded in a different manner.

As a centrally located institution with limited opportunities and resources for expansion, Georgia State College developed in 1959 a selective admissions program that contrasted sharply with its previous reputation as an open-door evening school. Under a court injunction not to discriminate against minority applicants and under state laws that: (a) limited the age of first-time college entrants and (b) withheld all funds in the event of court-ordered integration, Georgia State was, in many respects, the University System's "experiment station" for selective admissions. The admission procedures developed and followed from 1959 until 1965 are still instructive in their implications for institutions enforcing higher academic standards in the admission process.

In addition to the SAT, which was already required for entering freshmen, Georgia State applicants were required to take an extensive series of academic ability and educational achievement tests. Included in the "battery" of tests were measures of vocabulary, reading comprehension, and general achievement in natural science, mathematics, and social studies. Also required in the admissions process was an interview with a panel of three faculty members who made recommendations independent of the applicant's test performance. For admission as an entering freshman, only applicants who had followed a college preparatory course in high school were eligible. Four units in English and two units in mathematics, each with a "C or better" average grade, were mandatory.

The effectiveness of the new admission standards was documented in a doctoral dissertation by Thomas F. McDonald (1966). Statistically significant increases in SAT scores and high school averages were clearly evident, and appreciable improvement in academic performance was suggested by freshman grades. There were considerable variations in faculty grading practices, however, and the average grades recorded for introductory grades suggested persistence in faculty expectations of student achievement. In brief, the "rapid transition" to selective admissions had produced significant changes in student characteristics, but corresponding changes in faculty expectations and grading practices were not evident for several years. During the 1960s Georgia State changed in dramatic ways its institutional reputation and mission, but its success was not as much a function of selective admissions as its rapid expansion of degree programs to meet the increasing demand for higher education in a rapidly growing urban area.

Expansion of Georgia's Junior Colleges

In 1957 a special committee of the General Assembly studied the State's need for additional junior colleges and recommended the passage of legislation that would permit local government agencies to establish and operate new junior colleges. The ensuing Junior College Act of 1958 provided for a system of junior colleges that would be established and operated by local authority C and not as units of the University System. The Board of Regents, however, was authorized to adopt rules and regulations by which the local operating authorities would receive state aid (*Georgia Laws,* 1958 Session, pp. 47 50). DeKalb Community College, the only college established under the Junior College Act of 1958, received in its first years of operation a stipend of $300 for each student enrolled.

The enactment of the 1958 Junior College Act was a sharp spur to the Board of Regents in their commitment to the expansion of educational opportunity. Following studies of educational needs in Augusta, Savannah, and Columbus the Regents negotiated with: (a) the Richmond County Board of Education for the transfer of its junior college to the University System, (b) the city of Savannah for the transfer of Armstrong College, and (c) the Muscogee County School District for the creation of a new junior college. Thus Augusta College and Armstrong College, two previously established (and locally controlled) institutions, became units of the University System. One, Augusta College, had been founded in 1925 as a county-operated junior college while the other, Armstrong College, had an equally interesting history as a city-owned junior college founded in 1935 and housed in a historic Savannah mansion. The third unit, Columbus College, became the first newly established institution since the creation of the University System Center. The operation of the new colleges required a special allocation of $400,000 to the Board of Regents, and each entered the University System "by virtue of the authority of the Board of Regents" (*1958 Annual Report*) and not as instruments of the Junior College Act.

As the decade of the 1950s drew to a close, the institutional composition of the University System was: (a) four "comprehensive" institutions, (b) five senior colleges enrolling whites, (c) three senior colleges enrolling blacks, and (d) seven junior colleges. The addition of three junior colleges brought the total to nineteen units and the geographical distribution of institutions thereby increased educational opportunity.

The enrollment of 30,686 students had been restricted, however, by the passage of the Age-Limit Law of 1959. The law, passed without consultation with academic leaders, placed restrictions on the enrollment of undergraduates over 21 years of age and the admission of graduate students over twenty-five. The number of University System faculty members in 1960 was 1,512, an increase of 46 over the previous year. The average salary paid to teaching faculty on a nine-months contract was $5,973—an increase of 64.1 percent from the $3,639 paid in the academic year of 1949-1950. The University of Georgia, having conferred one Ph.D. in 1950, conferred 12 Ph.D.'s in l960, along with 8 Ed.D.'s; Georgia Tech conferred 12 Ph.D.'s that year.

If the immediate postwar years (1946-1950) are perceived as a period of readjustment in which the G.I. Bill was a dominant influence in a statewide quest for educational self-sufficiency, the 1950s can be regarded as years in which the University System also made progress toward educational respectability. Throughout the decade the University System's enrollments grew at an annual rate of 6.7 percent while the State's population increased from 3.4 million to 3.9 million (an annual increase of 1.4%). By 1960 the University System had an additional 12,269 students distributed among its various units. The increase in enrollments for the decade was 67 percent higher than the University System's enrollment in 1950.

In retrospect the postwar years of 1946-1960 should be viewed as a period of growth, expansion, and change in which commendable efforts were made to improve educational opportunities within the University System. The Regents and other state leaders were influenced by a changing "philosophy of education" that was expressed best by the President's Commission on Higher Education (1947). American colleges and universities were challenged to envision a larger and more significant role for higher education in the national life. Higher education was no longer a privilege for an intellectual elite but the means by which the nation's citizens could realize their individual potential for personal growth and development. From its perspective the commission was convinced that at least half of the nation's college-age youth could benefit from two years of college. To that end the commission addressed ways in which campus facilities could be expanded, technical institutes could be established, and college curricula could be improved.

A pronounced emphasis was placed on higher education as the means by which human talents could be discovered and developed. Testing and counseling were embraced as the means by which the various talents of students could be identified, appraised, fostered, and encouraged—and education was the means by which they could be developed and used. Guidance centers had proven effective for returning military veterans and many colleges followed suit in establishing offices of testing and counseling. A national interest in educational and vocational counseling (and placement) was thereby spurred—and with the passage of the National Defense Education Act of 1958, the discovery and development of talent was given the blessings and support of public policy. Accompanying this movement was an extensive national concern for college and university faculties, their formal preparation, working conditions, and their meager salaries. Many institutions responded with efforts to upgrade their faculties and to improve job benefits and working conditions. The gist of such changes was an increasing awareness of institutions, students, and faculties as public resources that required public attention and better financial support.

Chapter Four
Growth and Expansion: 1960-1972

Georgians today, whether or not they realize it, are fighting the educational battles of the 1970's. The outcome will depend largely upon their actions during the next two or three years. The outcome of the battles of the 1960's is already determined by the actions and inactions of the past.

Governor's Commission To Improve Education, 1963

The institutional composition of the University System changed dramatically in the 1960s, a decade of unprecedented growth, expansion, and progress. In 1964 the increased birthrate that began in 1946 was evident on all college campuses as eighteen-year-olds graduated from high school in unprecedented numbers and enrolled in college the following fall. Georgians were no exception to the national trend, and by the end of the decade neither the overall structure nor functions of higher education was the same nationally, regionally, or locally. Old institutions re-defined their mission and role. New institutions opened as rapidly as the construction of campus facilities would permit—and more than a few colleges began in temporary quarters while awaiting the completion of construction.

In December 1961 Georgia State was permitted to drop the prepositional phrase "of Business Administration" from its title and offer master of arts degrees in English, history, and political science. Also authorized at that time was a master of arts degree for teachers and a master of business education degree.

In 1963 new junior colleges were approved for Albany-Dougherty County, Dalton-Whitefield County, and Marietta-Cobb County. Approval of these three colleges was followed in 1964 by authorization of a fourth new college in Gainesville-Hall County. Beginning in 1963 the Regents began the upgrading of four junior colleges into senior institutions. Augusta College was granted permission to offer senior-division work in 1965, and Armstrong College would offer similar work in 1966. Both colleges were permitted to add additional years of academic coursework as an entering freshman class progressed in its studies. In this way, the junior year was added one year prior to the addition of the senior year. In early 1964 Georgia Southwestern was accorded the same privilege and was scheduled to offer upper-division work in 1966. During the 1964-1965 academic year Columbus College received permission to upgrade its status beginning in 1968 and conferred its first bachelor's degrees in 1970. As documented in a later doctoral dissertation (*Denning, 1972*), the four institutions were successful in their relatively easy transition to senior college status, but changes in institutional status were not as evident in student characteristics as they were in faculty credentials and program structure.

The status of the University System in the 1963-1964 academic year is significant because of the numerous changes that most institutions of higher education experienced in the fall of 1964 and the years thereafter. On June 30, 1964 the institutional composition of the University System was the same as it had been since the opening of Columbus College. During the academic year of 1963-1964, however, a total of 1,826 faculty members taught the full-time-equivalent of 30,575 students enrolled in nineteen institutions. For their teaching, University System faculty members received an average salary of $7,589, an increase of $217 over the previous year. The University of Georgia conferred 35 Ph.D.'s and 16 Ed.D.'s while Georgia Tech conferred 25 Ph.D.'s in several fields of engineering.

The dramatic increase in University System enrollments in 1964 was not unexpected, but it was not properly anticipated. Georgians did not participate in higher education at the same rate as residents of other states and although it was evident from high school graduation rates that more students were completing high school, it was not anticipated that a higher proportion of those graduates would enroll in college. In a two-year period (1964-65) the number of high school graduates increased almost 40 percent. No other event, perhaps, could have demonstrated so well the University System's need for statewide planning and development.

The number of freshmen entering the University System in 1964 was over ten thousand, an increase of at least 38 percent since 1960. The 1964 freshman class was the first of the postwar generation to enter college, and their better preparation was evident in the higher proportion who scored above 600 on the

SAT-Verbal or SAT-Mathematics scales. An appreciable increase was also observed in the mid-range (400-600) where the majority of entering freshmen were expected to score. At least 13 percent of the class entered with an "A" average in high school. Also evident in 1964 was the increased enrollment of minority students in the University System. Their relative participation did not increase, however, to the same extent noted for majority students.

Program Planning and Development

In 1961 the University System of Georgia agreed to co-sponsor with the Georgia State Department of Education and the Georgia Department of Public Health a study of the state's need for nurses and other paramedical personnel. Work on a statewide survey began in October 1961 and was concluded the following year in the same month. Included in the survey were twelve occupations regarded as essential to adequate health care for Georgia residents: (1) dietitian, (2) hospital administrator, (3) laboratory technician, (4) licensed practical nurse, (5) medical assistant, (6) medical records librarian, (7) medical social worker, (8) medical technologist, (9) occupational therapist, (10) physical therapist, (11) registered nurse, and (12) X-ray technician. The purpose of the survey was to determine present and future needs for such personnel and to evaluate the adequacy of educational and training programs for meeting those needs *(Fincher, 1962)*.

The survey was most effective in verifying the state's need for health care personnel. The demand for health and medical services was definitely increasing and there were critical shortages in nursing and paramedical occupations. Educational and training programs were inadequate to meet present needs and certainly could not meet future needs. Nowhere in Georgia were there programs for preparing dietitians, medical assistants, medical social workers, occupational therapists, or physical therapists. Personnel for the remaining occupations were variously prepared for their duties by an array of hospital schools, vocational schools, and public or private colleges.

Recommendations to the sponsoring agencies included the establishment of accredited programs where there were none, the improvement of inadequate or weak programs, and the fullest possible coordination of existing and future educational and training programs. To provide adequate health and medical care to its residents, the State needed an effective statewide system of recruitment and placement, better advisement and counseling services in its schools and colleges, and more effective policies for utilization of nursing and paramedical personnel.

The nursing and paramedical survey was favorably received. Directly related to survey findings was the establishment of the State Scholarship Commission as a means of providing financial aid to students enrolling in critical-need professional programs. Instead of responding merely to the nursing and paramedical needs documented for twelve specific occupations, the sponsoring agencies made recommendations to the General Assembly legislation that would provide a general canopy for state assistance. Also related was the development of the schools of allied health services at Georgia State and the Medical College, and intensified efforts on the part of the allied health fields, as they quickly became known, in recruitment and public relations. A later modification of state laws permitted the licensing of graduates from two-year collegiate schools of nursing. This change enabled University System junior colleges to establish nursing programs and contribute to the supply of professional nurses.

Regents Study of Higher Education

In April 1963 the Board of Regents authorized a statewide study of higher education in Georgia. Dr. S. Walter Martin, vice chancellor of the University System, was designated director of the study and chairman of a nine-member steering committee. Thomas W. Mahler, associate director of the Georgia Center for Continuing Education, was selected as associate director of the study. Six task forces were organized to consider: (1) the scope and functions of post-high school education; (2) junior colleges and area trade schools; (3) demographic forces affecting the demand for higher education; (4) the planning and coordination of junior colleges; (5) estimated costs and finances; and (6) educational programs for science, professions, and technology.

The task force on educational programs was asked to consider present and future needs for degree-granting programs. Its original charge was then broadened to include the state's resources and needs for institutional research and to maintain close liaison with the task force on scope and functions. Dr. Judson C. Ward, Jr., vice president of Emory University and former president of Georgia Southern, was appointed chairman.

An early announcement by Vice Chancellor Martin to the task force on educational programs was the news that Emory, Georgia Tech, and the University of Georgia would confer, in 1963, a combined total of 100 Ph.D.'s. The University of Georgia conferred 20 Ph.D.'s and 14 Ed.D.'s but its cumulative total of conferred doctoral degrees had not yet reached a hundred. Also among the initial findings was an urgent need for cooperation among the state's three doctoral-granting institutions but recognition that cooperation was not highly probable.

The Regents Study of Higher Education was discontinued in the summer of 1963 when Governor Carl Sanders commissioned the Governor's Commission To Improve Education. When relevant, the work of the Regents task forces was absorbed by the larger, more extensive, better-funded study. Thomas W. Mahler was appointed associate director of the professional staff assembled for the commission's purposes and would continue his study of higher education, as launched by the Regents. James L. Miller, Jr., director of research at Southern Regional Education Board (SREB), was granted leave to serve as director and Woodrow W. Breland, professor of education at Georgia State, was appointed associate director for elementary and secondary education.

Governor's Commission To Improve Education

The commission study authorized by Governor Sanders was the first comprehensive study of elementary, secondary, vocational-technical, and higher education in Georgia. An excellent professional staff and ample resources were made available for consideration and study of educational issues at all levels. Governor Sanders served as chairman of the Governor's Commission and placed the major emphasis of his administration on the improvement of education and the closing of educational gaps that embarrassed the state.

The commission adopted the goals stated by the SREB Commission on Goals *(1962)* and worked within the context of ten objectives specifically related to Georgia's educational needs. The objectives addressed the issues of improvement and equality in educational opportunity, minimum standards for public schools, balanced academic and occupational programs, the recruitment and retention of good teachers, the improvement of efficiency, a statewide television network, planning and research, and adequate financial support for public schools and colleges.

Representation on the commission was appreciative of social, economic, and cultural forces within the state. On the commission were two future governors of Georgia and one future president of the United States; a future lieutenant governor; several highly visible opinion leaders; and several future members of the Board of Regents itself. Although politics and race were much involved, the commission, much to its credit, kept its sights on its educational objectives.

The strongest recommendations in the report dealt with planning. The commission stated unequivocally that the "most important single prerequisite for educational improvement in Georgia [was] effective long-range planning" (p. 18). Such planning should be continuous and could not be the work of a single commission. For the Board of Regents, the report emphasized a "top priority need" for a research and planning unit to identify and define "long-range problems and needs" (p. 49). For the separate units of the University System there was a need for institutional research offices. For the University System as a whole there was a need for "comprehensive community junior college(s) . . . by which local and community needs should be met." These colleges "should be established on the basis of a statewide survey using the best criteria known . . . [and] on a priority schedule over a period of years" (p. 52).

The commission noted as one of its most difficult problems the relationships between community colleges and vocational-technical schools. The commission recommended continued jurisdiction by the Regents in areas where there were junior colleges and no vocational-technical schools but "memoranda of agreement" with the State Board of Education in areas where both types of institutions existed. Noting that junior colleges had already been approved for Albany, Brunswick, Dalton, and Marietta, the commission recommended joint experimentation with comprehensive community colleges in areas where neither vocational-technical schools nor junior colleges existed. A particular emphasis was placed on "close cooperation and coordination" between the two statewide boards of education. To this end, both boards should take immediate action "to accomplish whatever changes are necessary in policy, organization, and staffing" to devote to long-range planning. The boards, themselves, should meet jointly on matters of mutual concern.

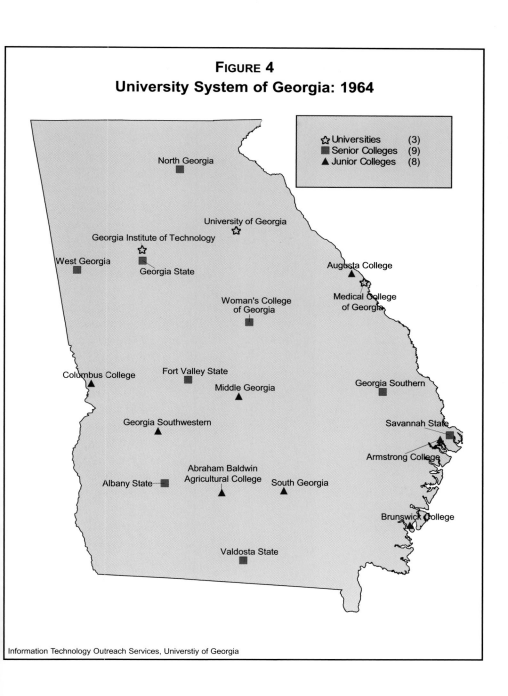

FIGURE 4
University System of Georgia: 1964

☆ Universities (3)
■ Senior Colleges (9)
▲ Junior Colleges (8)

North Georgia

University of Georgia

Georgia Institute of Technology

West Georgia

Georgia State

Augusta College

Medical College
of Georgia

Woman's College
of Georgia

Columbus College

Fort Valley State

Middle Georgia

Georgia Southern

Georgia Southwestern

Savannah State

Armstrong College

Abraham Baldwin
Agricultural College

Albany State

South Georgia

Brunswick College

Valdosta State

Information Technology Outreach Services, Universtiy of Georgia

A major emphasis, as would be expected, was on elementary and secondary education and the adequacy of their financing. The subtitle, "Investment in the Future", is indicative of the emphasis given education as an investment and the return-on-investment to society. Such an investment "will require full financial support from both state and local sources" and "every dollar's worth of wealth in Georgia should pay its fair share . . ." *(p. 72)*. The challenge called for "leadership of the highest order" and "educational innovation and experimentation."

In dealing with the state's efforts to attract space age industry, the commission recognized the tardiness of its major universities in organized research and graduate education. Attention was called to the state's shortage of scientific, professional, and technical personnel in areas of sponsored research related to the space age and to the need for "a generally higher level of educational attainment" *(p. 72)*. Basic research was acknowledged as "a function of the state's universities" but for reasons unknown, the commission's recommendations for graduate education are the weakest in its report.

The findings and recommendations of the Governor's Commission To Improve Education report were widely publicized and endorsed. Results were not always immediate but they were substantive. One significant outcome was the formation of the Georgia Educational Improvement Council, an intergovernmental agency consisting of representatives of the State Board of Education, the Board of Regents, the General Assembly, and private enterprise. Thomas W. Mahler was appointed the first executive director of this agency and continued many of the cooperative efforts initiated by, or recommended by, the Governor's Commission. When Governor Jimmy Carter decided to abolish this agency as an executive arm, the staff was re-assigned to the General Assembly as a legislative agency.

The urgency of the commission's work was dramatized one year later when the number of high school graduates in the state increased by 19.1 percent and an increased proportion enrolled in units of the University System. The year 1964, as often pointed out, was the first year of the "impending tidal wave" discussed by Roland B. Thompson of Ohio State in various national publications.

Other outcomes of the Governor's Commission report were less visible. The report and the Governor's Conference on Education, called to publicize the commission's findings, were undoubtedly effective in calling attention to educational needs and in committing more of the state's resources to education. What the work of the Governor's Commission demonstrated best, no doubt, was the need for effective leadership!

Regents Study of Community Junior Colleges

One important recommendation of the Governor's Commission was implemented the following year (1964) when the Regents directed the chancellor to conduct a comprehensive study of the need for additional junior colleges and to recommend their locations. This action was apparently triggered by the approval in March 1964 of Gainesville Junior College, which was the fifth junior college approved by the Regents since 1958.

In 1963 the Regents requested a study of the northwestern corner of the state that resulted in the approval of Dalton and Kennesaw junior colleges. That study was conducted in response to petitions from five different communities in the Seventh Congressional District for junior colleges and the Regents were obviously under the pressure of "planning by chambers of commerce."

The Governor's Commission responded to the particular issue, in effect, by saying the planning should be done on a systematic, statewide basis and as "a function of the Board of Regents." With this reminder of their responsibilities, the Regents responded by appointing an eight-member advisory committee which included representatives of Georgia colleges and universities who were well informed about national and regional trends in the development of higher education. Consultants for the study were B. Lamar Johnson from UCLA and I. E. Ready, head of the Community College Division of the North Carolina Department of Instruction. Staff directors of the study were S. Walter Martin, vice chancellor and later acting chancellor, and Harry S. Downs, coordinator of junior colleges in the University System.

The premises on which the study was conducted were: (a) equal and more-or-less universal opportunity for education beyond the high school; (b) acceptance of community colleges as comprehensive postsecondary institutions; (c) the essentialness of long-range planning; (d) Georgia's need for its own plan; (e) operation of community colleges by the Board of Regents; (f) a fixed role for community colleges as community colleges; (g) the need to identify communities and to recommend locations; (h) consideration of vocational-technical schools and their role; (i) the avoidance of needless duplication; (j) the study to serve as a foundation for future and continuing studies; (k) smooth articulation between schools and colleges, including community college/senior college transfers; and (l) the expectation that community colleges would increase rates of participation.

Among the guidelines established for the study were: (a) a potential enrollment of more than 400 students; (b) an acceptable concentration of population; (c) a commuting radius of 35 miles; and (d) community desire, interest, and ability to finance. Locations were to be assigned either a Priority A: "immediate development . . . seems justified," or a Priority B: "potentially promising [but] should continue to be studied. . . ."

The locations assigned a Priority A were four in number. To the study committee's satisfaction, community colleges were needed in the Bibb and Houston counties area, in the downtown area of Atlanta, on the west side of Atlanta, and in the south Atlanta area. Georgia State was identified as the logical institution to assume community college responsibilities in the downtown Atlanta area and Atlanta Junior College was the eventual outcome of the priority assigned western Atlanta. The Bibb/Houston priority, however, was an impediment in the study committee's report. Political commitments apparently had been made to Bibb County and the study committee was asked to make its recommendation specific. The study committee, believing the political commitment premature and thinking it had done enough in specifying the area, did not believe it could, in good conscience, recommend only Bibb County. Consequently, the final report was mimeographed only as a staff report for internal use by the University System.

Role and Scope Study of USGA Institutions

Another recommendation to which the Board of Regents responded was "a comprehensive study of the appropriate role of each institution within the University System and the appropriate scope of its activities" (*p. 50*). Such a study was launched in 1965 following the appointment of Dr. George L. Simpson, Jr. as chancellor. Dr. Walter Martin, vice chancellor of the University System, was designated study director and the Institute of

Higher Education at the University of Georgia, then in its second
year of operations, provided the staff work. The chancellor and
the Board of Regents requested that the study be concluded by
June 30, 1966.

The Institute staff defined the premises upon which a role
and scope study should be conducted and the information needed
from the separate institutions. There was agreement that: (a) the
demand for higher education would increase; (b) the majority of
Georgia college students would continue to enroll in the University System; (c) meeting the increased demand would require
both an expansion of academic programs and adequate planning
and coordination; and (d) all units of the University System must
assume a role that would be part of a larger whole.

An essential part of the study was the specification of general
guidelines under which institutional and program development
should take place. These guidelines were specified at the outset
and took into consideration the University System's need for
expanded educational opportunities that would be in keeping
with the resources of the State and the capabilities of its institutions. For examples, the Ph.D. should not be offered in any one
academic field at more than two universities and professional
programs (such as law, pharmacy, and social work) should be
significantly improved before diverting resources into new programs. The development of programs in the Atlanta and Athens
areas should be cognizant of their proximity, as well as the increasing concentration of the state's population. Other guidelines
dealt with considerations of the requirements of national and
regional accreditation, evidence of need and demand, and the
tri-fold mission of junior colleges.

In identifying the institutional role of each unit of the University System, a careful review of each institution's historical
development, the scope and diversity of its current programs,
and its institutional mission (as perceived by the president) suggested at least six functional institutional roles for the diversified
units of the University System. Four of the institutions already
served the major functions for which universities are traditionally
known; three of the senior colleges had a regional role (in their
provision of limited graduate work); five of the senior colleges
were limited in their efforts to define new roles by historical
traditions; three senior colleges (by virtue of their location) had

community ties that defined many of their responsibilities; and the junior colleges differed significantly in their community services and whether or not they attracted students from outside their immediate area.

A disappointing outcome of the role and scope study was the license taken by many institutions in projecting academic programs for future development. Student enrollments, full-time faculty, and credit-hours taught had shown a remarkable unevenness across institutions but the institutional aspirations of many units were inordinate. In short, the guidelines developed for the study could not curb the desires and preferences of administrative staffs and faculties.

Given its premises, its guidelines, and the cooperation of participating institutions, the role and scope study of the University System could have served as an informed guide to future institutional and program development. The six institutional roles defined in the study, however, were either politically or budgetarily unacceptable and despite sound caution in the study's conclusions and recommendations, the scope of academic programs under the canopy of institutional role was undoubtedly seen as opening floodgates of institutional aspirations already out of hand.

A long-range planning study began a few months after the role and scope study was completed. The staff work for this study was provided by members of the chancellor's central staff and each institution was asked to specify its own assumptions concerning enrollments, entrance requirements, academic programs, faculty, facilities, and other institutional activities. For example, an assumption made for the University of Georgia was that it would continue to enroll approximately 25 percent of the equivalent-full-time on-campus enrollment in the University System. Also assumed were such matters as the continued recruitment and retention of well qualified faculty, the expansion of research programs, and "a major break-through in graduate education."

Definitions were provided by the chancellor's staff for data elements that were to be projected for 1970-71 and 1975-76. Twelve categories were given for projections in educational and general expenditures while nine categories were given for educational and general income. For example, the FY75 E&G expenditures for the University of Georgia were projected to exceed one million

dollars, a tripling of its actual expenditures in 1965-66. As another example, the University of Georgia faculty was expected
to reach 1,500 in the academic year of 1970-71, a figure that was
attained at least two years earlier.

For the University System, the planning projections were put
to effective use in 1967 by Chancellor George Simpson in his
budgetary requests for the 1967-69 Biennium. In a public statement entitled, "A Dam Has Broken," Chancellor Simpson made
a persuasive appeal for funds that would permit the University
System to meet its obviously increasing obligations.

Policy Decisions in 1960-1972

The decade of the 1960s can be viewed as years in which the
State's first serious efforts were made in statewide planning for
higher education. The development of the University System
during the 1950s was commendable but piecemeal. No systemwide policies guided or directed the growth and expansion of
higher education, and too many policy decisions were made by
state legislators and other public leaders who proposed institutional and program changes to the Board of Regents.

The 1962 nursing and paramedical survey was the first statewide effort to plan and develop academic programs on the basis
of systematic research into the supply and demand of professionally trained personnel. The Regents Study of Higher Education
was the first concerted effort to view the total picture of higher
education within the state and to include representation of private
higher education on all six task forces. The Sanders Commission
To Improve Education was the only statewide, public commission to consider education from kindergarten to graduate school.
And the Regents Study of Community Junior Colleges was the
Board of Regents' first recognition that within its own institutions
could be found the knowledge and expertise needed to fashion a
plan for the orderly development of two-year colleges.

Despite the fact that decisions and commitments for Brunswick, Gainesville, Kennesaw, and Albany junior colleges had
been made in the early 1960s, their construction and development
were influenced by the concerted efforts to plan and direct the
growth of higher education in the 1964-1972 period. It is most
relevant that between 1964 and 1972, eight new junior colleges
opened their doors and provided additional access and educational

opportunity to Georgians in a period of rapid growth and expansion. Macon Junior and Clayton Junior colleges were undoubtedly proposed and approved as a result of the Regents Study of Community Junior Colleges. Although Atlanta Junior College did not open until 1974, it too was the result of planning carried out in the mid-1960s. In much the same manner, Floyd Junior College (although given a "B" priority in 1964) was an outcome of both the 1964 study and the earlier study of northwest Georgia. The approval of all three colleges had been made at a time *when* a climate for growth and expansion prevailed and *before* student protests in 1968 and 1970 resulted in a severe climatic change for higher education nationally.

The Board of Regents' commitment to the expansion of educational opportunity still prevailed in December 1970 when approval was given to six additional sites for junior colleges. It is relevant that the study by which the six new locations were identified was conducted internally by the chancellor's staff. The sites were: (1) Bainbridge-Decatur County, (2) Dublin-Laurens County, (3) Griffin-Spalding County, (4) Swainsboro-Emanuel County, (5) Thomasville-Thomas County, and (6) Waycross-Ware County. Approval was given on the basis that despite the escalation of four institutions to senior college status, the state's two-year colleges had continued to educate approximately 14 percent of all students enrolled in the University System. Also relevant were projections of continued increased enrollment during the 1970s and prospects of community readiness to fund and support junior colleges in the six locations. Bond issues for site acquisition and construction were defeated in Laurens County (February 1973), Spalding County (June 1971), and Thomas County (August 1973) but local support was forthcoming at the other three sites and resulted in Bainbridge, Emanuel County, and Waycross junior colleges.

Among the decisive changes in the 1960-1972 period was the desegregation of the University System's predominantly white institutions and the changing status and functions of Albany State, Fort Valley State, and Savannah State colleges. With the admission of Hamilton Holmes and Charlayne Hunter to the University of Georgia in 1961 the Board of Regents was no longer impaled on the horns of conflicting federal and state laws. The Regents and institutions of the University System would continue to be involved in court cases and federal regulations dealing with desegregation, but they were no longer subject to state laws that threatened institutional closure. With the passage of Title III of the Higher Education Act of 1965 (and other federal legislation of the era) the three public colleges for blacks received public endorsement of their mission and role as essential public resources. The nation's "predominantly black colleges and universities" were first identified as a national resource in a study by Earl McGrath *(1965)*, a former U.S. Commissioner of Education. McGrath's study was instrumental in creating a climate of public opinion in which institutional assistance was seen as being in the national interest.

Albany State, Fort Valley State, and Savannah State benefited in numerous ways from the changes in public policy. The presidents, deans, and faculties were increasingly involved in statewide conferences, inter-institutional meetings, and academic councils. For the first time they participated fully in administrative and academic decisions concerning the University System's development. Title III funds were particularly effective in helping the three institutions develop long-range plans, offices of institutional research, and campus information systems. With other federal and state funds, Title III was also instrumental in the improvement of undergraduate programs, the addition of graduate work, the professional development of faculty, the improvement of instruction, and the enhancement of student services. A special benefit, according to one study, was the opportunities provided for the professional development of institutional leaders *(Fincher, 1980)*.

Other significant events during the years between 1964 and 1972 were:

- ◆ the creation of the Georgia State Scholarship Commission and the Georgia Higher Education Assistance Corporation by the General Assembly in 1965;
- ◆ efforts to establish "special-help" programs for students not fully qualified for college coursework;
- ◆ special funds to university-level institutions to assist in the development of academic departments of distinction
- ◆ the adoption in 1967 of a new transfer credit plan and/or core curriculum;
- ◆ the addition in 1967 of several hundred new faculty positions that raised the University System total to 3,543 faculty members; and

◆ the escalation of Southern Tech to a four-year division authorized to confer a bachelor of engineering technology degree.

Regents' policies and decisions during the 1960s were influenced profoundly by the radical demands and expectations that characterized the decade. Unprecedented growth and expansion, the stimulus of federal legislation and financial assistance, the difficulties of accommodating massive enrollments, the disruptions of student protests,the growing dissatisfaction of private benefactors, and the waning of public support often obscured the substantive and enduring progress that was made during the decade.The Higher Education Act of 1965 was a positive and constructive force in the development of institutions, programs, and professional personnel. Without the stimulus and challenge given by federal legislation, the growth and expansion of educational opportunities would have taken other directions with a different kind of momentum.

In summary—from 1964 to 1972 the University System gained each year an additional 8,028 students, the equivalent of four junior colleges with enrollments of 2,000 students each. The average annual increase of 18 percent expanded enrollments to over 100,000 students by 1971 and to 108,779 students the following year. With the opening of Floyd Junior College in 1970, the University System consisted of 27 institutions of public higher education and educational opportunities were within commuting distance of 90 percent of the State's (4.5 million) population.

For many reasons—1964, 1968, and 1970 must be regarded as pivotal and traumatic years in American higher education. Student protests on Georgia campuses were relatively mild when compared to those in other states, but Georgia colleges and universities were undeniably affected. In particular the shock of student protests was severe for campus administrators, faculty members, and alumni who knew nothing of student dissent until it was reported on the evening news. In virtually all respects, the 1960s closed on a pessimistic note that contrasts sharply with the decade's initial enthusiasm.

The outlook for the University System in 1972 was not as encouraging or promising as it had been in 1960, *but* a larger and improved system of public higher education was in place and its institutions were much better staffed and equipped to serve the educational needs of Georgians. From the vantage point of "a new century" it is clearly evident that the University of Georgia and Georgia Tech were, indeed, gaining recognition for the progress they were making. It was also evident that all institutions with the University System had benefitted from the Higher Education Act of 1965 and other federal legislation of the decade.

Although the 1960s had begun in a "research revolution" and ended in a "management revolution', many observers and even critics could see advantages in both. Significant and substantive progress was made in higher education and especially in state-wide systems of public higher education.

Chapter Five
Reform and Consolidation: 1972-1984

Most of the people born during the "baby boom" years did not go to college. Now, many years later, those people are of middle age; and many of them are contemplating the advantages which a college education, if obtained even at this time, would confer on them. We witness a "greying" of the students at a number of our institutions.

Chancellor Vernon Crawford
1980 Annual Report

The year 1972 was indeed a decisive turning point in American higher education. The disruptive years of 1966-1972 severely undermined public confidence in higher education, its institutions, its faculties, and its students. From the heights of the early 1960s public opinion concerning the effectiveness of American colleges and universities descended to its lowest depths. With such change in public perceptions came drastic changes in public demands and expectations—and many changes in public policy!

The Educational Amendments of 1972 depict, in both subtle and obvious ways, the changing demands and expectations placed upon higher education in the aftermath of the 1960s. As a revision of the historic legislation of the mid-1960s, the Educational Amendments Act was both progressive and reactionary in its alteration of funding policies and practices and in its expressions of public perceptions, expectations, and concerns.

Among the many changes in public policy were forms of direct financial assistance for students that would permit students to enroll in institutions of their preference. Instead of supporting institutions and programs, in implementation of public policy, the amendments directed national priorities to basic and supplementary grants for "low income and minority" students. Other changes were equivalent to a redefinition of higher education as an instrument of national policy. Public higher education and private higher education were joined with vocational-technical

71

schools and proprietary institutions to comprise four sectors of postsecondary education.

Funding priorities were altered accordingly. Low income and minority students were designated as recipients of study loans, as participants in work-study programs, and as beneficiaries of special programs, such as Talent Search, Upward Bound, Special Services, and Educational Opportunity Centers. Title III (for developing institutions) remained intact as the only form of "general" institutional support but the criteria for Title III funds excluded the great majority of colleges. Throughout the amendments, policies and priorities emphasized planning, management, and evaluation. The clear implication of such emphases was the widespread belief that American colleges and universities have been mismanaged and that public policy should foster the adoption of modern management techniques in institutional operations.

Within the University System the early 1970s may be regarded as years of readjustment and accommodation, as well as years in which strenuous efforts were made to consolidate the gains of the 1960s. Having extended educational opportunity through the geographical distribution of institutions, the University System in the late 1970s sought extension of educational opportunities through program planning and development. As new and conflicting demands were placed upon its institutions of higher learning, the University System sought ways in which it could strengthen its programs and services for its many new constituencies and its diverse clientele.

During the 1971-1972 academic year Armstrong State, Augusta, Columbus, Georgia Southwestern, and Albany State colleges were authorized to offer graduate work at the master's level and North Georgia College was approved as a resident graduate center. In September 1971 authority for the operation of Gordon Military College was passed to the Board of Regents and in 1972 Gordon Junior College became the 28th unit of the University System. In the fall of 1973 Bainbridge Junior and Emanuel County Junior colleges raised the number of institutions to 30. In 1974 Atlanta Junior College became the 31st. During the same year a feasibility study for an additional college was conducted in Gwinnett County, a special committee was appointed to study tenure, and a new law school was authorized for Georgia State. Role and scope studies were initiated for senior institutions within the

System with expectations that a role and scope study would be conducted for the entire University System.

In 1975-1976 the Board of Regents placed a new emphasis on inter-institutional programs within the system and underscored quality and efficiency in the state's many health care programs. Kennesaw Junior College was authorized to upgrade its status to a senior college in the fall of 1978. A short-fall in projected state revenues resulted in a $24 million budget cut, however, and most institutions were hard pressed to handle an increase of 7.6 percent in cumulative enrollments of 173,212 students (*1976 Annual Report*).

In following years a School of Health Systems was established at Georgia Tech and a "three-two program" between Tech and Savannah State was initiated. The state's desegregation plan required a major overhaul in 1978, and the Board of Regents revised its policies for the Regents Test, special studies, and cut-off scores on the SAT. The changes in public demands and expectations are most evident, however, in the directions taken by the new chancellor in 1979-1980. Southern Tech was established as a separate unit of the University System and major task forces were appointed to consider: (1) the optimal distribution of institutions within the State, (2) admission standards for the various units, (3) academic advising as a much needed service to students, and (4) affirmative action.

Policies and Academic Standards

Efforts to serve ever increasing numbers of students, many of whom were educationally disadvantaged, and increasing concerns for the maintenance of academic standards led to major revisions in Regents policies during the 1970s. After experimentation with summer admissions-on-trial programs and summer programs for enrichment and development, the Regents approved in 1973 the provision of special studies programs (later known as developmental studies) that would begin in September 1974. Early in 1972 a passing score on the "Rising Junior Test" was officially established as a graduation requirement for students earning degrees in institutions of the University System. And in 1979 the Regents gave official approval to the core curriculum for freshmen and sophomores that had been initiated in 1967.

The University System's response to the challenge of educationally disadvantaged students is evident in systemwide tests of reading and writing for "rising juniors" and developmental studies programs to assist students unable to meet regular admission standards. As one of the nation's first statewide systems to adopt standardized tests (i.e., the Scholastic Aptitude Test), the University System was quick to see the advantages of a systemwide test in basic skills for students moving from lower division coursework to upper division fields of specialization.

The policy decision to require such tests in all units of the University System was made in 1969. The stated purpose of such tests was to assure senior institutions that transferring students met explicit standards of academic competence. One implication of the requirement was to give stronger emphasis to the basic skills of reading and writing in lower division coursework, especially freshman English courses. In the beginning, however, a passing score was not required for graduation.

The failure rate of the Regents Test (as the test was later named) has been discouragingly high. One fourth of the students taking the test for the first time fail to make a passing score. The failure rate varied, of course, from institution to institution and occasionally ran as high as 85 percent for some institutions. Fortunately, students taking the test for a second time had a passing rate higher than those taking the test for the first time.

Later modifications were made in the Regents Testing Program as one component of its desegregation plan. In a 1984 agreement with the Office of Civil Rights, the Regents improved significantly the assistance given students who had failed the test. Students in the historically black institutions were required to complete approximately 50 instructional hours of remediation before retaking the test. Assistance to such students included sessions in which test-taking techniques were discussed *and* a student/teacher ratio of no more than twenty to one in remedial courses. In addition, the institutions developed reading and writing laboratories that were coordinated with remedial instruction. The coordination of such instruction with developmental and freshman English courses assured the Office of Civil Rights that students failing the Regents Test would benefit from programs of assistance more comparable to the services provided entering freshmen.

The establishment of programs of developmental studies in 1974 was directly related to the knowledge and experience gained in the Regents Testing Program. Regents policies specified that each institution would have a separate department or division of developmental studies, with a separate budget and staff. Funding for the program was to be on the same basis as other lower division programs of study. To tie the program firmly to the academic administration of each institution, Regents' policies further specified that the chairman of each developmental studies program would report directly to the chief academic officer of each institution "or his/her designee."

Other matters addressed in Regents policies for developmental studies were entrance requirements, exit requirements, and course credit. Originally set as a combined SAT score of less than 650 and confirming scores on the College Board's Comparative Guidance and Placement Test, entrance standards have been modified by separate cut-off scores for the verbal and mathematics sections of the SAT and by the development of a basic skills examination by members of the Regents' staff. In 1988 admission to developmental coursework was modified further through the use of a Comparative Placement Examination (CPE) that was developed by the American College Testing Program. To exit developmental courses, students must satisfy criteria decided by their respective institutions.

The courses taught in developmental studies were specified as English, reading, and writing but are not limited to such courses. Regents policies thereby encouraged the separate units to be responsive to the special needs of students in matters of personal, financial, academic, and career counseling. In addition, all institutions are required to provide academic advisement to ensure that students are informed about developmental requirements. No degree credit can be awarded for developmental coursework but institutional credit must be! Students thus can earn up to 30 hours of credit in developmental studies and all such credits are transferable to other University System institutions. The grading system used in developmental studies courses is identical with other academic grades within the institution.

Given its many years of experience with developmental studies the University System is, or should be, in a good position to assess the effectiveness of instruction in basic skills for educationally disadvantaged students. Roughly 19,000 students enroll in developmental studies each fall and for two-year colleges the enrollment averages about 25 percent of the institution's total enrollment. Senior college enrollments average about 12 percent of their total enrollment. The magnitude of the University System's effort is shown by estimates that one out of three students take some kind of remedial work in their freshman year. Programs are evaluated in terms of student retention, grades received in later coursework, completion of degree requirements, and other criteria involving comparison with regularly enrolled students.

When asked (in 1982) to judge the effectiveness of their programs, over 60 percent of the directors of developmental studies rated their programs as "moderately successful." At least one out of three directors rated their programs as "highly successful" while no director regarded his or her program as unsuccessful. The responding directors estimated that at least 53 percent of their students successfully exited developmental studies and that 36 percent completed a regular college program *(Fincher, 1984)*.

Governor's Committee on Postsecondary Education

The Educational Amendments Act of 1972 firmly endorsed statewide planning in its Section 1202 provisions for statewide planning commissions. Because of its confusion of "planning" with "planning and coordination," Section 1202 was not funded as quickly as other sections of the 1972 act, and the appointment of "1202 commissions" was delayed in most states. Georgia's first 1202 commission, appointed by Governor Jimmy Carter, served quietly and with varying success for several years.

The decision to establish a separate public commission as the 1202 commission was advisable. Since Section 1202 provided for representation by four different sectors of postsecondary education—public higher education, private higher education, vocational-technical education, and proprietary education—there was an understandable reluctance on the part of the Board of Regents either to seek or to accept designation as Georgia's 1202 commission. For the same reason the State Board of Education could not be designated and a separate public commission was the only way in which to provide representation for the State's private and proprietary colleges.

In 1978 Governor George Busbee established a new 1202 commission with different and more specific responsibilities. To avoid confusion with the previous commission, he identified Georgia's 1202 agency as the Governor's Committee on

Postsecondary Education and appointed David H. Gambrell, former U.S. senator, as chairman. Other appointments to the committee were representative of the universities, senior colleges, and junior colleges in public higher education; universities and senior colleges in private higher education; public education at the elementary and secondary levels; the state's vocational-technical schools; proprietary education; and the state's business, industrial, and financial interests.

Governor Busbee defined the work of the committee as that of a problem-defining commission. He asked the group to "determine what the problems are, where our greatest needs lie, and what should be our priorities." The committee's response was given, one year later, in its report submitted to the governor. Entitled "Postsecondary Issues: Action Agenda for the Eighties," the report *(COPE, 1979)* defined ten major issues confronting postsecondary education in Georgia and suggested an agenda of ten statewide actions to be taken in resolving the defined issues. The issues themselves were stated in terms of statewide needs that concerned all sectors and levels of postsecondary education.

All sectors of postsecondary education were insufficiently recognized by the general public and better promotion of the state's diverse educational opportunities was needed. A comprehensive statement of postsecondary goals and improved communications (with better cooperation) among institutions was also needed. Issues should be identified before they become crises *and* an on-going process for identifying and analyzing issues should be established. The use of public resources should be more effective and efficient, and to this end the committee recommended better methods of assessing and reporting progress. A review of funding policies and processes was needed to ensure adequate funding and more effective budgeting. Taking note of widespread deficiencies in basic skills and the irrelevance (for later careers) of many postsecondary programs, the committee recommended a reconsideration of institutional responsibilities for teaching basic skills and a better balance in general and technical programs. To promote and to assure better cooperation among the four sectors of postsecondary education, an advisory commission for postsecondary education was suggested.

The state's need for a comprehensive statement of postsecondary goals and objectives was the issue delegated in 1979 to the second Governor's Committee on Postsecondary Education.

Governor Busbee appointed himself chairman of the Second Governor's Committee and sought essentially the same representation of sectors and interests in the appointment of other members. The committee staff remained intact.

The statement of goals and objectives submitted the following year to the governor was indeed comprehensive. But like the issues defined earlier, the defined goals and objectives contained no surprises. Eight general goals were identified and grouped under the rubrics of individual development, diversity and accessibility, institutional responsiveness and excellence, effectiveness and efficiency in the use of public resources, and public awareness. Subsumed under the eight state-level goals were a varying number of objectives designed to tie the goals more tightly to specific policies, actions, and results.

- The intellectual, ethical, personal, and educational development of individuals to enable them to live in an effective, responsible, productive, and personally satisfying manner.
- Comprehensive, diversified, and accessible postsecondary education opportunities for the citizens of Georgia.
- Equitable opportunity for individuals to participate in postsecondary education, consistent with their abilities and needs, without regard to race, sex, age, religion, ethnic origin, economic status, or handicap.
- Responsiveness by postsecondary education to changing needs of individuals and society.
- Excellence in administration, instruction, research, and service consistent with institutional missions.
- The effective and efficient use of resources by public and private institutions in meeting institutional purposes.
- Communication and cooperation among educational institutions, associations and agencies related to postsecondary education, business, industry, labor, and government.
- Public awareness and knowledge of the availability, quality, and benefits offered by all sectors of postsecondary education.

Upon reappointment in 1980, the Governor's Committee began a series of studies to assess the progress that was being made toward state-level goals and objectives in postsecondary education.

Neither the governor nor the committee had set goals and objectives for institutions, programs, or professional personnel. The committee had merely defined in one document the stated or implied goals of existing institutions or programs. The committee's work then became one of assessing the progress postsecondary institutions and programs were making toward those goals.

The Governor's Committee again rendered valuable service in its third year as a 1202 commission. The assessment of progress proceeded in various ways. Six doctoral students in higher education at the University of Georgia contributed doctoral dissertations to the committee's work. The dissertations were statewide surveys of interinstitutional cooperation, community services, honors programs for superior students, advanced placement and course exemption policies, student retention, and the reactions of corporate recruiters to college graduates from Georgia institutions. A seventh survey, not developed as a doctoral dissertation, dealt with student services.

In 1981 the Governor's Committee submitted its third report and, perhaps for the first time, conveyed the remarkable diversity of private and public postsecondary education in Georgia. An institutional inventory disclosed at least 308 institutions providing some form of education beyond the high school and worthy of the name postsecondary education. Within the state were: 34 public colleges or universities; 40 private colleges or universities; 30 public vocational-technical schools; 10 private certificate or diploma schools; and 206 proprietary schools, 10 of which were degree-granting.

Progress was clearly evident in the diversity of opportunities, but public awareness of postsecondary opportunities was another matter. The committee recommended a directory, inclusive of all postsecondary programs, and later published such a directory in tabloid form under the title of *The Bridge*. The publication of this directory continued in 1983 when Governor Joe Frank Harris released a third edition.

The committee, concluding from its various studies that the future of private education in Georgia was relatively secure, recommended that state assistance to students in private colleges remain at its relative level to per-student allocations in public institutions. Postsecondary institutions evidently were meeting the career needs of students but there were reservations about their responsiveness to changing demands. Academic, career, and personal counseling services were not readily available to many students and institutions were lax in meeting the demand for noncredit, part-time, special/remedial, nontraditional forms of instruction and training. Student financial aid was still inadequate, with too large a portion of it being federal funds only.

In December 1982 the Governor's Committee, continuing its work without federal funds, issued a report summarizing its work for the previous four years and recommending priorities in postsecondary education for the future (COPE, 1982). Addressing again the issue of student financial aid to private accredited institutions, the committee recommended the conversion of the state's Tuition Equalization Grant program to a needs-based program. Restated were its earlier recommendations of funding relative to University System per-student allocations and the inclusion of appropriately accredited proprietary schools. Added was a recommended proviso that financial aid should go only to students "able to benefit from postsecondary education."

Anticipating the work of several national commissions, the committee recommended that postsecondary institutions "clearly define their expectations of high school prerequisites . . . and assist high schools in meeting those expectations." Also recommended were more definite admission requirements for colleges. These requirements should be consistent with student abilities, as measured by standardized ability and achievement tests and previous academic performance. With respect to instruction in basic skills, the committee recommended that no degree, certificate, or diploma credit be given for such instruction and called upon colleges for "policy plans" that would eventually phase out all developmental studies programs.

Future concerns for postsecondary education in Georgia included: (a) the coordination of secondary and postsecondary efforts in the development of basic skills; (b) the low rate of participation in postsecondary education by Georgia residents; (c) the adequacy of student financial aid; (d) the improvement of funding and budgeting; (e) the governance of vocational-technical education; and (f) clearer definitions of institutional roles. The concluding section of the 1982 report again stated the public need for an advisory commission on postsecondary education with statutory authority.

Although the Governor's Committee was officially continued by Governor Harris until July 1983, the committee did not meet again and its fourth major report was its final report. The committee staff continued as an office under the new administration but consisted in 1984 of only the director and a senior planner.

Regents Desegregation Plan

In 1978 the Regents extensively revised their plan for desegregation by addressing more directly the elimination of duplication in business administration and teacher education programs at Savannah State and Armstrong State colleges. Operating under federal guidelines that fostered the preservation of institutional identity while removing vestiges of dualism, the Regents transferred to Armstrong State all undergraduate and graduate courses in teacher education at Savannah State. In similar manner they transferred to Savannah State all undergraduate and graduate programs in business administration at Armstrong State. Faculty members involved in the transferred programs were reassigned to the other institution. As part of the plan, the stipulation was made that appropriations for the two colleges would not be affected as a result of enrollment fluctuations.

The Regents plan was adopted at a time when similar considerations were underway in the cities of Nashville and Norfolk. The plan for Savannah differed, however, from the decisions made in the other areas by being the explicit plan of a governing board responsible for both institutions. In Nashville the merger of two somewhat similar institutions was ordered by a federal court, and in Norfolk joint planning for inter-institutional cooperation was mandated by state and federal officials.

In the first year of the implemented plan, enrollments declined at both Armstrong State and Savannah State. Other-race presence on the two campuses was noticeably increased by virtue of the conditions under which presently enrolled students could transfer. In both institutions students maintained an option of graduating with degrees conferred by the institution from which they had transferred. Other conditions of transfer assured that academic credit would not be lost and completion of degree programs would not be delayed. During the second year slight gains in total enrollments occurred at both institutions, but total gains were accompanied by slight declines in other-race enrollments.

The effectiveness of program transfer as a means of desegregation was not evident ten years later when an intensive consolidation study was conducted. Total enrollments at both institutions had declined from 1978 through 1987. In business administration programs the enrollment at Savannah State was significantly less than the combined enrollment at the two institutions ten years earlier. At Armstrong State an increase was observed for the total enrollments in teacher education, but the number of teacher education students who were black had decreased.

The success of the Regents' plan was more evident in the establishment of a joint continuing education program that was housed in downtown Savannah. The Coastal Georgia Center for Continuing Education now has its own conference facilities, benefits from an unusually favorable location in the historic district of Savannah, and continues to be jointly staffed by the two institutions.

Other features of the Regents' desegregation plan included an inter-campus unit for the administration of all joint efforts between Albany State and Albany Junior colleges, a "two-plus-two" academic program for the same two institutions, a criminal justice institute at Albany State, and other programs involving student incentives and distinguished scholars. The plan received "formal unconditional approval" by the Office of Civil Rights in March 1979.

Planning in the 1980s

In the early 1980s the Board of Regents addressed several major policy issues dealing with finance, the future of public higher education in the State, the potential uses of telecommunications in University System programs and services, the state's need for programs in the health professions, off-campus degree programs, and statewide assessment in nursing education. The University System of Georgia was re-affirmed as a statewide system of public higher education; the organization and function of its separate institutions were to be reviewed; methods of funding and financing were to be proposed; and continued growth and development were to be based on systematic inquiry and analysis.

Study Committee on Finance

In January 1981 the Board of Regents, the General Assembly, and the governor jointly appointed a Study Committee on Public Higher Education Finance. Appointments to the study committee were representative of the three sponsoring agencies, private higher education, and the state's business and professional interests. Staff work for the committee was provided by an independent, out-of-state consulting agency. The study committee adopted as guiding principles to its work: (a) the need to continue improvement of the quality of the University System; (b) the need for more efficient management; and (c) the need for a funding system that would provide incentives for quality improvement and efficient management. A more basic premise on which the committee began its work was the inadequacy of the funding formula that originated with the 1963 Governor's Commission to Improve Education.

The findings and recommendations of the study committee were presented in September 1982 by Governor Busbee to "All Georgians Interested in Higher Education." The major recommendations called for a more equitable sharing of educational costs and specified that student tuition should account for 25 percent of total revenue for general operations in the resident instruction budget. To attain this proportionate sharing of costs, tuition should be increased 15 percent annually until the 25 percent objective was reached.

To foster efficient management of institutional resources, the study committee recommended that institutions be permitted to carry forward unexpended funds for one year and use such funds for nonrecurring items such as equipment and library materials. Also recommended for the purpose of efficient management was the retention of 85 percent of indirect cost recoveries on sponsored research and other externally funded programs.

The funding formula recommended by the study committee specified major categories for: (a) instruction and research, (b) public service, (c) academic support, (d) student services and institutional support, and (e) plant operation and maintenance. For instruction and research, the committee recommended funding by lower division, upper division, and graduate levels and by five instructional or programs areas—corresponding roughly to behavioral and social sciences; professional and applied fields;

arts, sciences, and foreign languages; developmental education; and medicine, dentistry, and veterinary medicine.

Other details of the formula specified academic support at 17.7 percent of the funding base established for instruction, research, and public service; student services and institutional support at 23.1 percent of that funding base; and a special provision for quality improvement at one percent of the total budget. The proposed funding system would maintain Georgia's rank among the upper fourth of southern states and focus attention on strategies for quality improvement. No provisions were made in the formula for protecting institutions from declining enrollments and where enrollments did decline, the Regents were encouraged to examine carefully the continued need for those institutions.

The recommendations of the Study Committee on Public Higher Education Finance thus had many promising implications for the improvement of education. The quality improvement provision would create funds for faculty recruitment and retention, professional development programs for faculty, the development of special programs, and the purchase of special classroom and laboratory equipment.

Statewide Needs Assessment

In August 1981 the Board of Regents initiated "a comprehensive statewide needs assessment designed to provide a foundation for charting the course for public higher education in the state." The resulting report, "The Eighties and Beyond: A Commitment to Excellence," was the most relevant statement on public higher education in Georgia since the report of the 1963 Governor's Commission To Improve Education. The statewide needs assessment was conducted within the span of one year and was rightly expected to provide a basis for planning and development within the University System. The objectives of the Regents study were: (1) to analyze current programs of instruction, research, and service—and to identify additional services that should be provided; (2) to determine if the present complex of institutions is sufficient for meeting identified needs; and (3) to project changes that will be necessary in the foreseeable future.

Noting that the success of the University System in the 1960s and 1970s was judged in terms of growth, the needs assessment report declared the improvement of educational quality to be the measure of success in the 1980s. The first recommendation in the report called for establishment by the governor, General Assembly, and Board of Regents of quality improvement as the top priority for public higher education. The report endorsed the study committee on finance's report as "one of the most significant documents in the history of the University System" and recommended its full implementation *(p. 19)*. The introduction to the report referred to the study committee on finance's report as a significant companion document.

Having declared quality improvement as its top priority, the coordinating committee for the study recommended: (a) closer cooperation between the Regents and the State Board of Education; (b) creative partnerships with community, business, and industrial leaders; (c) a system of program evaluation with both internal and external efforts; (d) a long-range goal of eliminating developmental studies; (e) the reinstitution of specific academic requirements for admission to units of the University System; and (f) a systemwide program of faculty development.

Concerning the structure or institutional composition of the University System, the coordinating committee recommended that no changes be made in present institutional structure or status. Existing institutions were to be carefully monitored, however, to determine if declining enrollments implied closing or consolidation. In the meantime, better use was to be made of cooperative residential doctoral programs, telecommunications, and satellite research centers to deliver needed services. The Board of Regents was expected to study its institutions in Albany and Savannah and to determine if their present structure served the needs of their respective areas and the state as a whole.

A major strength of the University System was identified as its governing structure and the leadership it could provide. The Regents, therefore, were to set priorities for institutional and program development and to make those priorities known. They were to take a more direct hand in the definition of institutional missions and ensure that institutional missions supported the University System as a whole. The Board would continue to delegate to institutions the autonomy they required for diversity and academic excellence, but the Board should readdress the problem of institutional service areas and refine its guidelines so as not to encourage unhealthy competition.

Other recommendations to the Board of Regents included: (a) strengthening the periodic review of institutional productivity and management; (b) studying institutional and program duplication with an eye to consolidation; and (c) measuring institutional productivity in terms of academic excellence, as well as the usual quantitative indices. In accomplishing these recommendations the board should also strive for better communications with both the citizens of Georgia and their elected representatives in the General Assembly.

Recommendations concerning institutional and/or program matters were directed to: (1) the liberal and fine arts, as the core of instruction in each of the units; (2) agriculture, as a highly specialized and scientifically oriented industry; (3) business, industry, and technology, as significant partners in the creation of economic wealth and well-being; (4) the medical and health professions, as a cluster of particularly important service occupations; (5) teacher education, as a profession requiring close study; (6) research, as a function requiring continuing overall commitment as an essential part of the University System's mission; (7) public service and continuing education, as functions and responsibilities with increasing importance, and (8) public and social services, as areas of community need that are subject to change.

The Regents Needs Assessment Report closed with a cogent statement of the University System's role and functions as "a cohesive and coordinated response to the public higher education needs of the state" and a nod in the direction of its next fifty years of service. Reaffirmed was its commitment to the "basic operating principle articulated by the first Board in 1932—the responsibility to determine what will best serve the educational interests of the state as a whole."

Other Systemwide Studies

The advent of the adult learner and other nontraditional students was an unheralded blessing on many college campuses nationally and within the state of Georgia. In many uncalibrated ways the increased demand for higher education by older students, new students, and part-time students was the salvation of many colleges during the 1970s and the 1980s. During the 1980s alone the traditional college-age population (18-24 years) of the nation declined 15 percent while the population of adults (25-44 years) increased by 20 percent.

As a systemwide study in 1983 disclosed, adult learners within the University System averaged 31 years in age and almost one-half of the group was 30 years of age or younger. This finding suggested that adult learners in Georgia's public colleges were not so much adult learners as they were returning students or late-starters. Almost two out of three of the group were women, and an overwhelming majority were white.

The secondary preparation of adult learners in the study compared favorably with that of many other "traditional students" within the University System. The high school average of the adult learners was a substantial "C" average, but a larger proportion of the group had high school grades below average. With respect to their performance on the SAT, adult learners scored appreciably lower but not in ways that were unexpected. As a group, they scored at a creditable level on the verbal section of the SAT and at a lower level on the mathematics section. More noticeable differences were observed in the higher verbal scores of women and the higher mathematics scores of men. The same differences were observed in a subgroup who had not completed high school. Despite the discontinuance of their secondary schooling at an early age, the adult learners in the study scored acceptably well on a standardized test of academic ability and met, with reasonable satisfaction, the course requirements and faculty expectations of institutions within the system.

Classroom performance, as reflected in freshman grades, was related to the adult learners' reasons for continuing their education, the type of program in which they enrolled, and the level of the institution in which they were enrolled. A major finding of the study indicates that adult learners, like many transfer students, may experience difficulty during their first quarter of enrollment but their academic performance improves significantly with classroom experience *(Fincher, 1983)*.

Another systemwide survey in 1986 found that the admissions data presented in the annual norms booklets is often used in unpublicized ways by administrators, faculty, and staff who are involved in academic decision making. Most relevant, perhaps, is the finding that the admissions data collected annually have many uses not directly related to admission decisions. High school counselors are among the most frequent users of SAT scores in helping high school students identify colleges to which they might apply. After admissions, test scores and high school grades may be used for academic awards or other forms of student recognition prior to the earning of freshman grades. In all cases, however, the uses of such information are always in conjunction with other information that has been gathered on students.

Other effective uses of the SAT were found in academic placement, class sectioning, academic advising, personal counseling, and in institutional research and planning. SAT scores do not appear to be used widely, however, in the evaluation or assessment of academic programs. The predictive efficiency of the SAT has been the subject of several doctoral dissertations within the State's universities. All such studies reflect the SAT's usefulness and effectiveness in predicting grades but suggest that the SAT's major value is the information it provides about student abilities and achievement *(Fincher, 1986).*

Policy Decisions in 1980-1984

In the early 1980s many challenging policy decisions were placed on the Board of Regents' agenda. Policy changes requiring attention were recurrent issues, such as changes in institutional status and the geographical distribution of educational opportunity in graduate education. Other major decisions were needed in areas of policy related to the state's commitment to academic excellence *and* to equity or fairness for the University System's changing constituencies. The size and complexity of 34 diverse institutions educating over 120,000 students challenged the governance capabilities of the Board of Regents, as well as the administrative competence of institutional leaders.

Procedures and guidelines for cooperative programs were approved in 1980, and opportunities for participation in doctoral programs were extended to senior colleges working in cooperation with the University of Georgia and Georgia State University. In similar manner, cooperation between units of the University System and institutions outside the system were encouraged under policies permitting the establishment of joint programs. Programs in the health professions continued to expand and to require new forms of cooperative agreements with clinical agencies and organizations.

In December 1980 the board adopted a policy statement concerning procedures for determining the feasibility of changes in institutional mission and status. Three colleges were seeking university status, and a fourth was seeking elevation to the level of senior college. Other policy statements adopted by the Board of Regents in the early 1980s dealt with academic advisement and with basic requirements for the University System's core curriculum.

In January 1981 the Regents adopted the recommendation of the Georgia Public Telecommunications Task Force that the system's public television station be placed under the authority of a newly created Public Telecommunications Commission. One of the reasons given for the Regents' decision was the "opportunity" to work more closely with the State Board and State Department of Education.

Following a recommendation of its Task Force on Optimal Distribution of Institutions, the Board adopted a more "functional classification" of institutions in which: universities were classified as either comprehensive (Category A) or special purpose (Category B); senior colleges were classified as either senior college (A) or special purpose (B), and junior colleges were Category A (offering transfer and career programs) or Category B (offering transfer, career, *and* vocational-technical programs).

In 1983 the Regents adopted a revised policy manual in which efforts were made to eliminate inconsistencies and to reflect more accurately the numerous changes made in systemwide policies. Among the new policies included in the revised manual were: (1) provisions for external degree programs, (2) changes in the academic calendar for the University of Georgia law school, (3) revisions in policies concerning developmental studies, and (4) revisions in the University System's tenure and nontenure policies.

Policy issues on the Regents' agenda in 1983-1984 were: (1) college participation rates and ways in which institutions could increase participation, (2) ways in which DeKalb Community College could become a unit of the University System, (3) agreements with the State Board of Education that would implement Governor Joe Frank Harris' establishment of "a third board" for postsecondary vocational-technical education, (4) adoption of a pre-college curriculum requirement for admission to the

University System, and (5) evidence of "substantial progress" in meeting the state's desegregation goals. Initiated during the year was a formal procedure for the review and improvement of teacher education programs not having a 70 percent passing rate on the state's Teacher Certification Test (TCT).

In summary, the University System in the early 1980s reached a level of notable maturity. Its fiftieth anniversary was quietly observed and passed unnoticed by the news media and the great majority of its constituents. Thirty-three institutions of higher education served well the needs of Georgians for undergraduate, graduate, and professional education. The unspoken goals of self-sufficiency and respectability had long been met, and plans for geographical distribution had been implemented well. The respective institutions and their faculties were in quest of national recognition, and noticeable progress was evident in many institutional commitments to excellence. The diversification of institutions and programs was an acceptable, if not complete, match for the pluralistic needs and preferences of the system's constituencies. Progress had been made in minority access and equity, women were the majority students in many classes and in some institutions, and adult learners were enrolled throughout the system. Certain problems did persist, however, as 40 percent or more of the University System's entering freshmen scored in the lower third of the nation's high school graduates in basic skills of literacy. Far too many could not read, write, or reason as well as previous generations of college students. And despite the effectiveness of developmental studies, too many graduates left the classrooms of colleges and universities with lingering deficiencies in basic academic competencies.

With the 1980s came new challenges, demands, expectations, and needs. As the separate institutions coped with changing demands and expectations, their success was varied and uneven. The momentum gained in twenty years of rapid growth and expansion was commendable but difficult to sustain. Once again, the University System was called upon to lend its institutions, programs, and talents to the solution of societal problems and the resolution of complex issues in public policy. The Board of Regents' agenda was increasingly crowded with matters of national and regional urgency, as well as the internal rivalries of ambitious and energetic institutions.

CHAPTER SIX
Review and Coordination: 1984-1992

If we learn from the past but are not captive to it, we are more likely to have the ability to build a vision for the future that, when realized, will lead to making right those things that are wrong, making better those things that are good.

Chancellor H. Dean Propst
System Summary, 1990

B) eginning in 1985-1986 the University System obtained, for the first time, full funding of the revised "formula for excellence" recommended by the 1982 Study Committee on Public Higher Education Finance. The new chancellor noted in his annual report "the constructive working relations that have been forged between the Board of Regents and the Board for Postsecondary Vocational Education." A study conducted by the Southern Regional Education Board did *not* support the state's need for a second engineering school and, to the contrary, presented evidence that Georgia Tech was not adequately supported in providing engineering programs that had long served state and national needs.

The status of the University System in 1986 was evident in an equivalent-full-time enrollment of 113,685 students and a total enrollment of 135,964 students. A total of 24,040 degrees and certificates were conferred, and at least 6,199 faculty members, making an average salary of $31,039, were involved in teaching, research, and service. Over 12,550 continuing education programs had a total of 472,730 participants.

The institutional composition of the University System was again changed in 1986 when DeKalb Community College became the 34th unit. Since 1964 DeKalb Community College had been the only junior college established under the Junior College Act of 1958 and the only public institution of higher education that was *not* under the jurisdiction of the Board of Regents. In the same year Clayton Junior College was advanced to senior college status and re-named Clayton State. In many respects the changing status of the two colleges brought to completion a network of institutions in the Atlanta area that was discussed in 1964 by the Regents Study Committee on Community Junior Colleges.

Further changes in the system's composition followed in 1988 when the state's junior colleges were permitted to drop the word "junior" and select a title more in keeping with their varied missions. As part of a general effort to facilitate the effectiveness of two-year colleges in meeting community needs, the chancellor had appointed in 1987 a study committee, chaired by President Derrell C. Roberts of Dalton Junior College, to make recommendations concerning the mission and roles of Georgia's public two-year colleges. The committee concluded from its study that mission statements should re-affirm the public two-year colleges as "an essential part of Georgia's statewide system of public higher education," and expand the means and locations by which students earn degrees. Five major roles for two-year colleges were defined as the provision of: (1) general education; (2) lower division coursework that would transfer to senior colleges; (3) instructional and developmental courses for inadequately prepared students; (4) career-related programs that required college-level instruction; and (5) service programs and activities for their respective communities.

Respondents to the committee's survey were confident that two-year colleges could provide high quality transfer programs and yet be comprehensive in the programs and services they offered. Despite funding differences between the two, academic programs of instruction and continuing education programs were regarded as fully compatible. Respondents were unanimous in their belief that the differences between two-year colleges and other postsecondary institutions should be emphasized and more adequately publicized.

Survey findings and committee recommendations were submitted to the Board of Regents in November 1986. In addition to the changes in institutional names, the Board of Regents approved at a subsequent meeting differential admission standards that would permit the colleges to distinguish between applicants seeking vocational or technical training and academic coursework for transfer to a four-year institution.

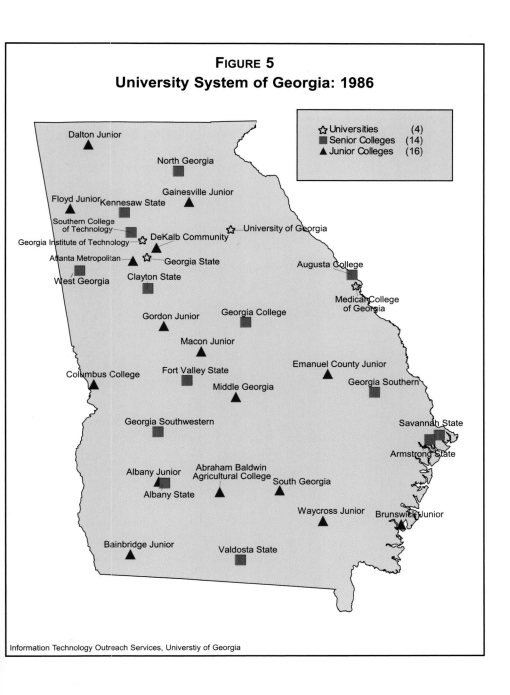

FIGURE 5
University System of Georgia: 1986

☆ Universities (4)
■ Senior Colleges (14)
▲ Junior Colleges (16)

Dalton Junior

North Georgia

Gainesville Junior

Floyd Junior Kennesaw State

Southern College of Technology

Georgia Institute of Technology

DeKalb Community

University of Georgia

Atlanta Metropolitan

Georgia State

Augusta College

West Georgia

Clayton State

Medical College of Georgia

Gordon Junior

Georgia College

Macon Junior

Columbus College

Fort Valley State

Emanuel County Junior

Middle Georgia

Georgia Southern

Georgia Southwestern

Savannah State

Armstrong State

Albany Junior

Abraham Baldwin Agricultural College

South Georgia

Albany State

Waycross Junior

Brunswick Junior

Bainbridge Junior

Valdosta State

Information Technology Outreach Services, Universtiy of Georgia

Assessment and Accountability

Policy and program decisions in the late 1980s were increasingly concerned with institutional effectiveness and accountability in meeting the changing demands and expectations of the University System's constituencies. The assessment of academic programs had been a policy issue throughout the 1970s. Federal legislation and regulations gave an impetus to program evaluation and other funding agencies had followed their lead. In 1977 a subcommittee of the Administrative Advisory Council had been appointed to study ways in which the assessment of academic degree programs could be facilitated within the University System. A survey by the subcommittee revealed considerable readiness within the system to assess and to evaluate academic programs, but a decided preference for local norms and internal standards was expressed by most respondents. Appreciable consensus was found in the need of institutions for methods of program assessment that would help determine the direction of future program development.

The subcommittee, accepting the survey findings as the basis for its work, directed its further efforts to the development of a rationale whereby program assessment within the separate institutions would lead to the improvement of undergraduate instruction while maintaining institutional autonomy or independence in deciding program content and academic standards. In its report the subcommittee clearly stated the difficulties of program assessment in a statewide system as varied as the University System of Georgia. Neither program objectives nor outcomes could be uniform *at* university, senior college, and junior college levels and *across* the diverse academic departments of the different institutions.

The subcommittee report recommended options and alternatives whereby departments of instruction would accept responsibility for the assessment of all programs in which departmental staffs decided course objectives and requirements. To meet its responsibilities in assessment, each department should define the program to be assessed, specify the methods of assessment used, and report all findings and conclusions to academic officials. A definite option open to each department was the selection, adaptation, or construction of assessment instruments that would serve their particular purposes. Among the many alternatives suggested to departments were formal or traditional methods such as standardized tests, semi-formal or structured techniques such as the use of outside examiners and simulation exercises, and informal means such as internships, apprenticeships, etc. The subcommittee's intent in developing a rationale and suggesting departmental options was to engage the academic departments themselves in the active assessment and evaluation of learning outcomes. The reactions of several departments, however, was to the contrary. Many faculty members saw the assessment of student learning, by means other than course grades, as an evaluation of teaching effectiveness. As the result of faculty resistance and other conditions at the time, exit examinations were unevenly applied as a means of program assessment and as evidence of institutional accountability.

Among the conditions fostering accountability in the 1980s was a returning concern with inter-institutional cooperation and working agreements with other state agencies having responsibilities in the various sectors of postsecondary education. In cooperation with the State Board of Education, the Regents established higher admission standards for students entering units of the University System. For applicants planning to enroll in degree programs (leading to a baccalaureate), four units of high school English, three units of science, and three units of mathematics would be required in the fall of 1988 and thereafter. Also included in the requirements were three units in social science and two units in a foreign language. As admission requirements, the courses were regarded as minimum standards for successful performance at the college level. As customary in establishing systemwide policies, all units of the University System retained the right to set higher, but not lower standards.

In raising admission standards for the entire system the Regents were influenced significantly by the College Board's definition of basic academic competencies that are needed in virtually all areas of college coursework. To publicize its new admission standards the Regents published an attractive brochure in which the "essential courses and skills" were identified and discussed in terms of their relevance for educational achievement. Following the first year of implementation, a doctoral dissertation *(Albright, 1990)* disclosed that completion of the college preparatory curriculum in high school was indeed predictive of academic success at the college freshman level. When other factors such as SAT scores and high school averages were controlled, the effect was small but nonetheless statistically significant *and* promising.

Other forms of cooperation were seen in the creation of the Board of Technical and Adult Education. Established first by executive order as a board of postsecondary education and later receiving statutory status under the Quality Basic Education Act of 1985, the new state board sought ways in which associate degrees could be offered in the state's technical schools. The potential for conflict was obvious in the career programs of junior colleges and the need for fundamental or general education courses in the associate degree programs of technical schools. Cooperative agreements between the two boards thus were essential to the effective operations of their respective institutions. In many ways the situation was reminiscent of the conditions studied by the Governor's Commission To Improve Education in the early 1960s.

Educational and training programs for the health professions was another area in which conditions were reminiscent of earlier years. In 1985 the Georgia Student Finance Authority funded an extensive needs assessment study of over twenty-five health professions within the state. Documented in that study were severe shortages of personnel in nursing, occupational therapy, and physical therapy. Less severe shortages were found in allied fields such as radiological technology and the laboratory sciences. The supply of educated and trained personnel was not sufficient to meet the demands of health care institutions. Nursing, in particular, was a profession requiring special attention from the Regents Committee on Health Education (*Morris, 1987*). Once again, the recurrent concern for the education of health professions personnel dealt with limited supply and increasing demands in health and medical care.

Regents Administrative Development Program

An important feature of the 1984 revision of the Regents desegregation plan was the provision of an administrative development program for minority faculty members. The program began in the fall of 1984 and continued for three years until 1987. Under the conditions of participation in the program, faculty members within units of the University System were nominated by their presidents and selected after an extensive interview with members of the chancellor's staff. The interview served both to inform the nominees about the objectives and procedures of the program and to assess their readiness for an intensive program involving seminars, workshops, and internships over a nine-months period.

Selected participants began their internship by attending a two-week seminar conducted at the Georgia Center for Continuing Education in Athens. The seminar was taught by the staff of the Institute of Higher Education and an option for participants was two hours of graduate credit as inservice education. The substance and content of the two-week seminar was an overview of higher education in the nation and state, an indepth look at the University System of Georgia and its various institutions and programs, and an intensive discussion of administrative concepts and principles. Following the seminar the Regents Fellows reported to the supervising administrator with whom they worked during the academic year. By observing, studying, and participating in administrative decisions, the Regents Fellows were exposed to administrative duties and responsibilities in an unusually effective manner. They were also exposed to University System policy decisions by attending a meeting of the Board of Regents and (with their host president) a meeting of the University System Advisory Committee. Interviews with the chancellor and his staff were also scheduled for each participant, as part of his or her observation and study of the University System.

In the winter quarter the Regents Fellows returned to Athens for a two-day workshop with experienced academic administrators. In the spring they closed out the year with an intensive, week-long evaluation workshop in which they reviewed with their colleagues their activities and experiences. At the end of the workshop each participant evaluated the overall program, including the formal and informal aspects of the year's activities.

The effectiveness of the Regents Administrative Development Program has been assessed in a doctoral dissertation written concurrently with the program (Booth, 1987). Twenty-six faculty members participated in the program and at least nine of them were involved in a significantly higher level of administration a year after completing their fellowship. Other participants benefited from the program in other ways, and none regarded the program as a waste of public or personal resources. Individual benefits were matched by various benefits to the institutions at which the Regents Fellows served. The extent of participation is further indication of the program's effectiveness. Over twenty different units of the University System participated in the program as either a home or host institution.

In 1987-1988 the Regents Administrative Development Program was extended for a year in a provisional effort to assist recently appointed administrators within the University System. Presidents were asked to nominate deans, directors, or department heads who had recently assumed administrative responsibilities and who would be interested in participating in a developmental workshop prior to the opening of the fall term. Nominating institutions were responsible for the travel expenses of participants and for such support as they might be able to give a developmental project that each participant would conduct during the year. The Institute of Higher Education was responsible for the opening workshop in the fall and for a closing workshop in the spring.

The quick response to the chancellor's request for nominations resulted in two fall workshops, one in August and another in September after several administrators had assumed new duties. Each fall workshop was similar in format and substance to those conducted for Regents Administrative Fellows. At the spring workshop in 1988, twelve of the fall participants presented papers that had been organized and written during the past year.

An Assessment of the System

In 1987 President Noah Langdale of Georgia State University was asked by the chancellor to undertake an in-depth assessment of the University System, its current status, and its prospects for the future. Included in the chancellor's list of charges were 25 issues, problems, and concerns that were within the purview of the Regents' control and authority. The study was concluded two years later and presented to the Board of Regents on December 13, 1989.

The scope of the assessment study was a "retrospective and prospective examination" of the University System. The rationale by which the study proceeded was the coalescence of President Langdale's experience as president for thirty years with the related experiences of other well informed, actively involved participants in the University System's growth and development since the 1950s. Working with President Langdale were W. Lee Burge, former chairman of the Board of Regents; John W. Hooper, former vice chancellor of the University System; and Cameron Fincher, director of the Institute of Higher Education. Assisting in the study were the presidents of the 34 units and numerous vice presidents, deans, directors, or department heads who submitted reports on the diverse institutional functions under their supervision.

In its coverage of varied and complex issues, the assessment report conveys the scope and the complexity of the problems with which institutional leaders in public higher education must cope. Policies, programs, and problems were considered as part of more complex, more significant events taking place at national, regional, and state levels. By presenting historical, national, and regional perspectives, the report brought out many distinctive features of Georgia's system of higher education and identified many common policy issues, which all institutions and statewide systems must effectively resolve.

The report discusses a dozen or more driving forces that facilitate or impede the progress of the University System. Among these forces is the "ageing" of the system's institutions, facilities, faculties, programs, and services. Having succeeded in its many efforts to fulfill educational needs and public expectations, the University System became, in many respects, "a victim of its own success" with new and different competitors for public resources. As demands for educational services increase, the University System will be strongly challenged to renew and to enhance its resources and capabilities. Other driving forces are national purposes and objectives, as seen in the influence of public policy and federal legislation; continued access and equity for minority groups, as seen in the national push for integration and equality; and a returning concern for "the basics, classics, and ethics" as institutions in the University System cope with the increasing cultural diversity of their students. Accompanying (and often countering) these forces are public indifference, technological obsolescence, over extended specialization, widespread tendencies to trivialize, and a failure to honor (in education) what we seek to promote.

In many functions and activities, the report noted, there is far more data collected and distributed than information or knowledge. Within several institutions there is more emphasis on pragmatic results than the liberal arts. In teaching and instruction there is often more concern with "partial success" and "extrinsic rewards" than excellence and personal satisfaction. And in fulfilling institutional responsibilities, more attention is given to "cost-cutting" efficiencies than to the development and appreciation of human competence or proficiency.

An unusually valuable contribution to the report was made by the presidents of University System institutions. In responding to the policy issues with which the assessment was concerned, presidents of the various units provided insights and perspectives that must be considered in the future development of the University System. As a group, they were seriously concerned about public perceptions of higher education and the "erosion" of public confidence in the quality and relative value of college instruction. They were aware of declining academic standards but believed that the state's leaders in higher education could, if encouraged, address the issue satisfactorily. They were in agreement that "non-applicable studies" should be eliminated from college curricula, but they did not expect developmental studies to be eliminated in the foreseeable future. The declining pool of high school graduates will have an adverse effect on higher education, and efforts must be made to reduce dropouts in secondary education. In matters of staffing and organization, they were not worried about student/faculty ratios, "surplus educational capacity," administrative staff replacements, or federal regulations; they were worried about acute faculty shortages in selected academic disciplines. Thus, they regarded faculty salaries as "perhaps the most serious need" in the University System, and they would like to see "more flexibility" in administrative salaries to permit recognition of merit. In the maintenance and replacement of physical facilities and instructional equipment, presidents did not regard "present funding mechanisms" as adequate. Inflationary library costs are "a dilemma" and preclude the most effective use of library resources. In their recruitment, enrollment, and employment of minorities, the presidents expressed disappointment. They expressed further disappointment in their retention of minorities after successful recruitment.

The assessment report concluded with a detailed discussion of the observations made during the assessment study. Included in the observations are numerous suggestions for consideration by the chancellor and the Board of Regents. Explicit in the assessment report is the need for a statewide commitment to higher education that involves the cooperation of state government. Such a commitment is dependent upon the creation of "a

climate of urgency" and the assistance of institutional constituencies in making a unified effort to support higher education. If
the University System's financial needs are to be met, past budgeting practices, such as enrollment-driven formulas, will not
suffice and "extraordinary funding" will be necessary.

Higher education, the report noted, is often criticized for its
"order-taking" attitude and for its inclination to measure "what
can be measured." The former leads to indifference in institutions
of higher education and the latter leads to the corollary that "what
cannot be measured" is unimportant. In the assessment study,
no "posture for change" was readily found, and when educational
reform became a topic for consideration there is a tendency to
seek either simplistic or totalistic solutions. Yet, assessment and
accountability are "dominating terms" in higher education and
institutions must answer national criticisms. The report takes
special notice of the challenge to public higher education by the
"privatization" of government functions and by private schools
that are profit-driven.

The Board of Regents was urged to take a stronger interest in
undergraduate education and its improvement. Excessive compart-
mentalization of the curriculum and its resulting "trivialization
of academic subject matter" should be avoided. Whenever possible, the differences between pragmatism and the liberal arts
should be reconciled and a balanced undergraduate curriculum
should be one of the Regents' continuing goals. The need for
curricular change in schools of business and education posed a
special challenge. The former are challenged to prepare graduates
for competition in a global economy while at the same time protecting and preserving our natural environment. The latter is torn
between pressures for further professionalization and demands
for more subject matter content.

The University System was challenged to find ways in which
teaching faculty could be recognized and rewarded. Alternative
salary schedules should be sought in which effective classroom
performance could be maintained by skilled professionals who
establish student/faculty relations that are conducive to learning.
To this end, the Board of Regents should review policies involving annual faculty evaluations based on the "going market
rate." If current market rates are a factor in the intended salary
schedule, that fact should be explicit.

The report endorsed presidential leadership and authority in matters of institutional operation and urged the Regents to "make a stronger definition" of all administrative responsibilities. In the area of planning, however, the report notes abundant evidence of plans and scarce evidence of planning results. The Board of Regents was encouraged to require that all plans for improvement be accompanied by specifications for each plan's implementation.

With respect to assessment and other forms of evaluation, the report calls attention to the use of outside experts in the surveys conducted by Works and Strayer, the stimulus of legislative committees and public commissions in the 1950s and 1960s, the federal mandate of 1202 commissions in the 1970s, and more recent deferences in the use of outside consultants in major policy decisions. Implicit in many of the report's observations is the advice that the Board of Regents not relax its guard on the board's independence. The assessment report itself is evidence of what can be done internally, and a direct implication is the continued strengthening of the chancellor's staff for more comprehensive responsibilities in assessment and evaluation.

Regional Universities

In July 1990 the institutional composition of the University System was again changed by the escalation of Georgia Southern to university status. The concept of a multi-campus regional university had been proposed in 1989 as part of a systemwide effort to develop a strategic plan for public higher education in the state. The original plan included Georgia Southern, Armstrong State, Savannah State, Brunswick, and East Georgia colleges and the Skidaway Institute of Oceanography, all of which are located in the southeastern corner of the state. The rationale for the formation of a regional university included a "solution" to the "Savannah problem" of program transfer, institutional merger, and inter-institutional cooperation. Each of the institutions would gain better control of its internal operations and thereby preserve its particular heritage. Each institution would also achieve certain academic goals dependent upon expansion of their degree programs. Establishment of a multi-campus university also would eliminate artificial barriers existing among the institutions and decrease their rivalry for students in selected academic fields.

More importantly, the proposed university would expand educational opportunities for the region and give the region a more prestigious institution that could serve its particular needs. In addition, the proposed university would respond to previous efforts to establish a university in the southern half of the state.

Following approval of the concept by the Regents in January 1989 and a more intensive study of the mission and role of regional universities, a revised proposal for the establishment of regional universities was submitted in September 1989 by the Planning and Oversight Committee of the Board of Regents. The approved proposal established a Type I (regional) category to correspond with the other two categories for funding university-level institutions and set the date for Georgia Southern's change-of-status to a regional university, with the participation of Armstrong State and Savannah State. The mission of the new university was to offer a more comprehensive array of baccalaureate degree programs, a wider range of master's and Ed.S. programs, and extensive programs at the doctoral level. The research programs of the regional university would be carefully differentiated from those of the other four universities. The term "regional" was used to specify a mission that was less-than-statewide in nature.

Georgia Southern College officially became Georgia Southern University, with further designation as "a regional university of the University System of Georgia." In addition to being units of the University System, Armstrong State and Savannah State are officially designated "an affiliate of Georgia Southern University." Each institution maintained its autonomy as an undergraduate college but participated in the graduate and research activities of Georgia Southern. All undergraduate degrees are awarded by the respective colleges and graduate degrees are conferred by Georgia Southern University.

Administrative titles of the three presidents were changed to include status as a provost of Georgia Southern University as well as president of their respective institutions. In other words, the president of Savannah State held the titles of president of Savannah State College *and* provost of Georgia Southern University. The president of Georgia Southern University also became the chief administrative official for graduate instruction and research. Day-to-day operations, however, are the responsibility of a new position called university vice president and dean for graduate studies and research. Among the new vice president's responsibilities is the chairing of a university graduate council and a university research council. To assist in the coordination of graduate programs, associate deans were based on the Armstrong State and Savannah State campuses. The graduate faculty of the new university consisted of faculty members (with appropriate credentials) at all three institutions. Thus the new university structure and functions intended coordination in graduate studies and research, provided a more comprehensive array of educational services in the Savannah area, and involved all three institutions in providing such services to the region.

In retrospect, the closing years of the 1980s should be regarded as one of the University System's most challenging stages of development. Within the brief span of two years, the presidential leadership of the system's three largest institutions changed and in rapid order major changes was again made in the system's major structure and functions. The changes observed in institutional status and leadership, in public and institutional policy, and in educational programs and services were both immediate *and* long range challenges to the Regents and the 34 institutions they govern. The way in which the University System responded to these various challenges is indicative of a level of maturity that was not evident in the 1950s and 1960s. The manner in which the University System itself fostered a systemwide assessment, a new university, a long-range plan, and a new budgeting process recalls the recommendations made in 1963 for strengthening the central organization and administration of the Board of Regents and for emphasizing "cooperative study, long range planning, coordination, and public advocacy of the needs of higher education." To borrow the words of President Emeritus Noah Langdale, the University System closed the decade of the 1980s, "in good condition, well led by its Chancellor, and with its interests, hopes, and promises well guarded by its Regents" *(p. 56)*.

Planning for the 1990s

In June 1990, with the awareness of the 20th century's last decade, the Board of Regents approved a comprehensive plan for the University System's continued development. The plan was the culmination of numerous studies, committee reports, and policy decisions that addressed the status and functions of public higher education in the 1980s. As its title indicates, the plan focused on the continuing and new demands that would be placed upon the University System and its contents gave good direction and guidance to the 34 institutions that would respond to the changing needs and expectations of the University System's many constituencies.

In responding to the needs of the state's growing population and its continuously developing economy, the plan gave good attention to the educational programs that prepare college students for productive, useful, and satisfying careers in agriculture, education, business, science, technology, and public service. As a statewide system of public higher education, the University System had unique responsibilities for the human resources that would be needed in the 1990s and in the early years of the 21st century. In responding to public demands and expectations, the plan addressed a statewide need for increasing participation in higher education. Recommendations in the plan thus dealt with ways in which: (a) students can be reached at earlier levels of education, (b) the participation of nontraditional students can be increased, (c) the retention and progression of students can be improved, and (d) the participation of minorities can be increased in all facets of public higher education.

A valuable and instructive feature of the plan was the mission statement given for the University System and the institutional roles defined for universities, senior colleges, and two-year colleges. The overall mission of the University System was simply "to promote higher learning and to advance and create knowledge." The system accomplished that mission through its 34 institutions, their respective faculties and students, and the application of knowledge "to the state as a whole." The system's performance would be measured by participation in its programs, services, and activities; by the impact of its programs and services; and by the efficiency with which they are provided. Among the University System's more immediate goals are a higher national ranking among its peers, status as a leading force in the state's economic development, and excellence in its graduate programs and research.

In defining the broad, general roles of comprehensive, special-purpose, and regional universities, the plan endorsed the comprehensive university's responsibilities for graduate education, professional education, baccalaureate programs, research, and public service. The doctoral programs established by regional universities should be in areas of specialization that are fully compatible with institutional mission and responsive to the demands of the communities served by the institution. Their emphasis should be on practical or applied forms of research that address regional problems and issues.

The baccalaureate programs of senior colleges should not be as comprehensive as those of the public universities, and the emphasis in faculty research should be discipline-oriented with results that are relevant to instructional effectiveness. When graduate programs are approved, they should be confined to work at the master's level in high demand areas of specialization such as business and education.

The programs of the two-year colleges are identified in terms of their relevance to other units of higher and postsecondary education. The focus should continue to be on the first two years of academic coursework for transfer credit and in preparation for advanced studies at another institution. Two-year colleges should also continue to cooperate with technical institutes in programs where general education requirements must be met. And for the foreseeable future two-year colleges were expected to be the primary provider of developmental studies for students who are inadequately prepared for higher education.

In brief, the plan's mission and role statements give valuable instruction and guidance to institutions in program planning, development, and assessment. The roles of institutions are differentiated by level of organization and by the scope or range of their multiple functions and/or purposes. Implicit in the differential roles of the 34 institutions are the many complementary ways in which they serve the larger, more significant purposes of a responsive system of public higher education.

Continuing education and applied research are two special areas in which the University System can contribute directly and substantially to the development of the state's economy and to the development of communities within the state. Other ways in which the University System can respond to the needs of state and society are:

1. extending baccalaureate programs into areas where access to college instruction has been limited;
2. meeting more effectively the needs of students for vocational, technical, and/or career-related programs of instruction and training; and

3. differentiating and coordinating the institutional roles that have been defined in the University System's structure of five universities, fourteen senior colleges, and fifteen two-year colleges.

A special, if not imperative, feature of the plan is its concern with the assurance and improvement of quality in programs, students, and faculty. The improvement of undergraduate education was, as stressed throughout the 1980s, the University System's greatest challenge and the coalescence of better prepared students, highly competent faculty, and well organized academic programs was the most demanding function of institutional leadership. Related to the improvement of undergraduate education is the need for better coordination in graduate and research programs. Both graduate instruction and applied research, as institutional services, are increasingly subject to the same pressures that decentralized many aspects of undergraduate education during the 1970s and 1980s. Further challenge is seen in the University System's growing concern for evidence of institutional effectiveness. As public demands for accountability increase and as accrediting agencies place additional emphasis on the assessment of educational outcomes, assurances of improved institutional effectiveness become mandatory for all institutions of higher education.

CHAPTER SEVEN
Progress and Continuing Development: 1990-1998

Over the next three years, our goal is to achieve full implementation of our strategic plan. We will see better prepared students coming into the University System, ready to do college-level work, and more students graduating from our colleges and universities who will remain in the state to work in jobs that we have helped to create.

Stephen R. Portch, Chancellor
1998 Annual Report

The decade of the 1990s opened with a highly optimistic outlook for the University System of Georgia. The population of Georgia had grown significantly throughout the 1980s and at least one additional representative in Congress was assured by the 1990 Census. Population projections indicated that within the first four or five years of the decade, Georgia would exceed North Carolina in population and become the nation's tenth largest state. Other demographic trends, such as the age, gender, and ethnic composition of Georgia's population, suggested that the state's social, economic, and political "growing pains" would not be as severe as those expected in other states. With such expectations, the University System of Georgia's status and potential for continued growth was indeed the result of its historical development, and its institutions, programs, and personnel do indeed reflect the fundamental importance of time, place, and origin.

In the fall of 1990 enrollments within the University System increased to 180,447 students. The relative gain in enrollment was 4.7 percent and when converted to full-time-equivalent students (n=6,026), the gain was still a substantial 4.2 percent. The relative gain for the University System, as a whole, exceeded in number of students the enrollments of all but three of the state's senior colleges. Relative increases in the junior and senior classes were appreciably higher than those observed in freshman classes. The highest relative gain, however, was at the sophomore level (14.6%). Twenty of the system's 34 institutions reported their highest enrollments of record and only four institutions within the System reported decreases in enrollment.

Over four out of ten students (43.6%) were enrolled in one of the system's five university-level institutions; slightly more than a third of the students (34.6%) were enrolled in one of fourteen senior colleges, and approximately one out of five (21.7%) were enrolled in one of the fifteen two-year colleges. When the class levels of the 180,447 students are considered, roughly one-fourth (24.5%) of the group were freshmen, less than one out of five (19.3%) were sophomores, one out of eight (12.2%) were juniors, and one out of seven (13.6%) were seniors. The remaining students were enrolled in graduate programs (13.0%) and professional degree programs (2.1 %), classified as "all other" (4.0%)—or enrolled in developmental studies (11.5%). The enrollment in developmental studies represented almost one in every twelve University System students.

The University System's approved budget for the fiscal year 1990-1991 exceeded 1.7 billion dollars, an increase of almost 100 million over the previous year. Included in the budget were salaries for 9,425 faculty positions, 2,175 research positions, 5,308 public service positions, and 2,460 administrators or professional staff members. Institutional budgets for the five universities ranged from 334.8 million for the University of Georgia to 60.7 million for Georgia Southern. For the senior colleges the average institutional budget was 22.0 million dollars while the average for two-year colleges was 8.85 million.

In summary, as the decade of the 1990s opened the University System included 34 institutions of higher education, employed the full-time-equivalent of 27,529 individuals as faculty and staff, enrolled at least 180,447 individual students, and expended 1.7 billion dollars in providing its numerous and various programs, services, benefits, and advantages.

Growth and Changing Status

The status of the University System's institutions, facilities, faculties, students, programs, and services in the fall of 1998 was further evidence of its potential for continued growth and

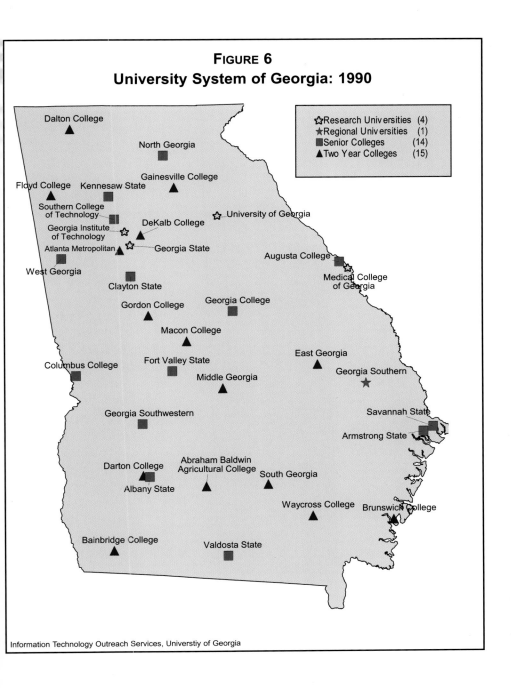

FIGURE 6
University System of Georgia: 1990

☆Research Universities (4)
★Regional Universities (1)
■Senior Colleges (14)
▲Two Year Colleges (15)

Dalton College

North Georgia

Gainesville College

Floyd College   Kennesaw State

Southern College of Technology

Georgia Institute of Technology

DeKalb College

☆University of Georgia

Atlanta Metropolitan

Georgia State

West Georgia

Augusta College

Medical College of Georgia

Clayton State

Gordon College

Georgia College

Macon College

East Georgia

Columbus College

Fort Valley State

Middle Georgia

Georgia Southern

Georgia Southwestern

Savannah State

Armstrong State

Darton College

Abraham Baldwin Agricultural College

South Georgia

Albany State

Waycross College   Brunswick College

Bainbridge College

Valdosta State

Information Technology Outreach Services, Universtiy of Georgia

development. January 1,1998 marked sixty-six years of remarkable progress and service by sixteen institutions with founding dates prior to 1932. Only eleven of the sixteen, however, can claim direct descent from an ancestor on the same site. In name, location, basic structure, and general functions, five institutions were comparable to their 1932 antecedents. The University of Georgia was still the state's largest and most comprehensive institution of higher education and Georgia Tech remained the state's primary technological or engineering institution. The Medical College of Georgia's title, of course, still conveyed its primary mission. Two colleges—Middle Georgia College in Cochran and South Georgia College in Douglas—were residential two-year colleges in 1932 and they retained that distinction in 1998. All other institutional comparisons between 1932 and 1998 reflect different paths, routes and perhaps several detours.

In the mid-1990s the University System of Georgia was in the fortunate position to benefit from the synergistic effect of a progressive governor, a cooperative Board of Regents, strong allies in the General Assembly, and the dedicated leadership of out-going and in-coming chancellors. Also contributing to the University System's good fortune was a favorable state economy, a climate of optimism concerning Georgia's future as state and society, a technological revolution in communications, and the international visability of Atlanta, Georgia as the site of the 1996 Summer Olympics.

In 1994 the Regents launched a strategic planning process, complete with a vision statement entitled "Access To Academic Excellence for the New Millennium", well stated "Guiding Principles" for strategic planning at both system and institutional levels, and a firm commitment to mission review and policy development involving their thirty-four institutions of higher learning. By 1998 the groundwork had been laid for a dramatic re-structuring of the University System as a statewide system of public higher education and as a remarkable resource for the state's educational, social, economic, cultural, and *political* advancement.

MISSION AND ROLES: The specific functions of the 34 units of the University System are generally depicted by their classification as universities, senior colleges, and two-year colleges. In a previous national classification of institutions *(CFAT, 1987)*, the University of Georgia and Georgia Tech were classified as major research and graduate universities. Both institutions meet standards in funded research, graduate programs, library holdings, and other assets that identify the two of them as national, as well as regional and state, resources. Georgia State was classified as a doctorate-granting university (Class I) and enjoyed an enviable reputation as one of the nation's leading urban universities. The Medical College of Georgia was classified as a specialized institution (i.e., a medical college awarding most of its professional degrees in medicine). Georgia Southern was classified at the time as a comprehensive college (Class I) but would soon become a doctorate-granting institution.

On the basis of their enrollments (over 2,500 students), graduate work (leading to a MA degree), and bachelor degrees (conferred in two or more professional fields) seven colleges— Armstrong State, Augusta, Columbus, Georgia, Kennesaw, Valdosta State, and West Georgia—were classified as comprehensive colleges (Class I). In meeting similar requirements in baccalaureate programs but not necessarily in graduate work, Albany State, Fort Valley State, Georgia Southwestern, North Georgia, and Savannah State colleges were classified as comprehensive colleges (Class II). None of the public senior colleges were classified as liberal arts colleges because their course offerings are not restricted to four-year programs in the arts, sciences, and humanities.

All of the public two-year colleges were classified simply as "two-year community, junior, and technical," with no distinctions made between Brunswick, Bainbridge, and Dalton colleges (with their vocational-technical programs) and other two-year institutions within the system. Variations in size were more pronounced among the two-year colleges than their respective roles within the University System. DeKalb College, with an enrollment exceeding 12,000 students, remained the largest and Waycross College was identified as the smallest.

By the fiscal year of 1999, when the semester calendar began, the names and classification of twenty-eight institutions had been altered to reflect changes in their mission and role as units of the University System. The names of *four* research universities (The University of Georgia, Medical College of Georgia, Georgia Institute of Technology, and Georgia State University) and *three* two-year residential colleges (Middle Georgia College, South Georgia College, and Abraham Baldwin Agricultural College) remained the same.

REGIONAL UNIVERSITIES: (n=2)

Georgia Southern University
Valdosta State University

PREVIOUSLY KNOWN AS

Georgia Southern College
Valdosta State College

*****

STATE UNIVERSITIES: (n=13)

Albany State University
Armstrong Atlantic State University
Augusta State University
Clayton College & State University
Columbus State University
Fort Valley State University
Georgia College & State University
Georgia Southwestern State University
Kennesaw State University
North Georgia College & State University
Savannah State University
Southern Polytechnic State University
State University of West Georgia

PREVIOUSLY KNOWN AS

Albany State College
Armstrong State College
Augusta College
Clayton State College
Columbus College
Fort Valley State College
Georgia College
Georgia Southwestern College
Kennesaw State College
North Georgia College
Savannah State University
Southern College of Technology
West Georgia College

*****

STATE COLLEGES: (n=2)

Dalton State College
Macon State College

PREVIOUSLY KNOWN AS

Dalton College
Macon College

*****

TWO-YEAR COLLEGES: (n=10)

Atlanta Metropolitan College
Bainbridge College
Costal Georgia Community College
Darton College
East Georgia College
Floyd College
Gainesville College
Georgia Perimeter College
Gordon College
Waycross College

PREVIOUSLY KNOWN AS

Atlanta Junior College
Bainbridge Junior College
Brunswick College
Albany Junior College
Emanuel County Junior College
Floyd Junior College
Gainesville Junior College
DeKalb College
Gordon Junior College
Waycross Junior College

In brief, the mission and role of each institution reflected its historical development within the University System. Institutions that began as a private, county, or city-sponsored college was changed to blend their respective responsibilities with those of other units of the system. There are noticeable variations in traditions and other institutional characteristics, but each institution serves well as an integral part of the overall system. Together the 34 institutions offer an impressive assemblage of educational programs, services, and activities. The University System itself is well described as a comprehensive statewide system of public higher education.

RESOURCES AND FACILITIES: The revenues and expenditures of the University System reflect the scope and magnitude of its numerous functions, operations, and activities. In FY 1998 the University System received $1.43 billion (38.0% of its total budget) in state appropriations and generated $524 million (13.9%) from student tuition and fees; $1.04 billion (27.6%) from gifts, grants, and contracts; and 768 million (20.4%) from other sources.

Sixty-nine percent ($2.65 billion) of the FY98 budget was expended on general operations. Included in such expenditures were academic support and student services (9.1%); institutional support (12.7%); physical plant operations and maintenance (5.5%); and the three major responsibilities of instruction, research, and public service—for which almost half (41.8%) of the University System's total funds are expended. Also included in the FY98 budget was $563 million (14.9%) for scholarships and fellowships: 249 million (6.6%) for auxiliary enterprises, and $316 million (8.4%) hospitals and clinics.

In keeping with its statewide presence, the University System's many physical facilities are dispersed throughout the state. If all classrooms, libraries, laboratories, dormitories, cafeterias, gymnasiums, health services, administrative and faculty offices, and other campus buildings could be reassembled in one location, they would occupy 1206 acres—slightly less than 14 percent of the total acreage that comprises the campuses of 34 institutions. The total number of all such buildings is 2,852 and their value has been estimated as five billion dollars. Two-thirds (69%) of the buildings are located on or controlled by the research and regional universities; state universities account for 597 (21%) buildings and state or two-year colleges operate with 310 (11%) of the buildings used for public higher education. Not included

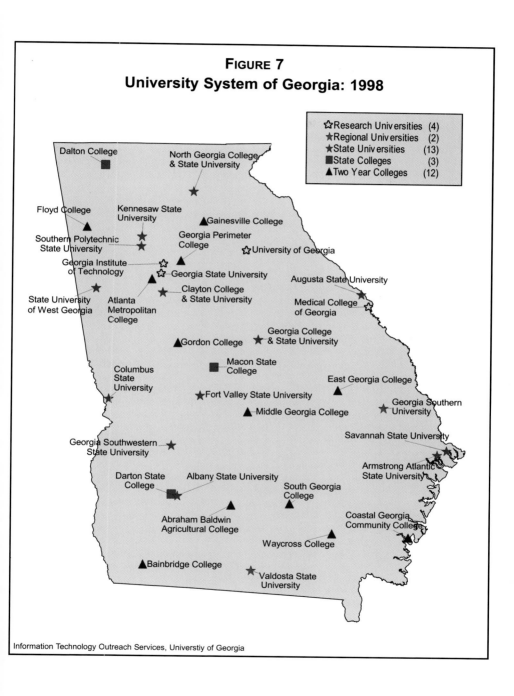

FIGURE 7
University System of Georgia: 1998

☆Research Universities (4)
★Regional Universities (2)
★State Universities (13)
■State Colleges (3)
▲Two Year Colleges (12)

Dalton College

North Georgia College & State University

Floyd College

Kennesaw State University

Gainesville College

Southern Polytechnic State University

Georgia Perimeter College

University of Georgia

Georgia Institute of Technology

Georgia State University

Augusta State University

Clayton College & State University

State University of West Georgia

Atlanta Metropolitan College

Medical College of Georgia

Georgia College & State University

Columbus State University

Gordon College

Macon State College

East Georgia College

Fort Valley State University

Middle Georgia College

Georgia Southern University

Savannah State University

Georgia Southwestern State University

Armstrong Atlantic State University

Darton State College

Albany State University

South Georgia College

Abraham Baldwin Agricultural College

Coastal Georgia Community College

Waycross College

Bainbridge College

Valdosta State University

Information Technology Outreach Services, Universtiy of Georgia

in the campus acreage are 45,696 acres located off campus and used primarily by the University of Georgia (43,334) and Fort Valley State (1,338), the state's two land-grant institutions.

When uses of physical facilities are considered, almost 38 percent of the floor space is used for academic and/or instructional purposes, 6.0 percent is used for administrative reasons, less than two percent is used for faculty and student support services, and the remaining 37 percent is used for innumerable "other" purposes (such as service buildings, rental property, parking decks). When the academic/instructional uses of physical facilities are considered, the University System uses 2,593 classrooms and 5,108 research laboratories, plus 125 other rooms for continuing education. Laboratories are classified as teaching labs (19%), non-teaching labs (19%), and research labs (62%). The recency of the University System's rapid growth is shown by the fact that 1,135 (40%) of its 2,852 buildings are less than twenty-five years old. Sixty buildings, however, are over ninety-nine years old and 90 buildings (4%) are over seventy-five years old.

In its quest for academic excellence, one of the University System's best investments can be observed in its campus libraries. Almost $103 million dollars were spent in FY98 on acquisitions, and total holdings in books, documents, and microfilm exceeded 36.6 million. The value of library holdings within units of the University System exceeded 382 million dollars. Over seven out of every ten books (72%) are in university system libraries of the four research universities. In 1989 the University of Georgia library contained almost three million volumes and was ranked 23rd among the nation's libraries; in 1998, UGA's holding exceeded 3.4 million, and the Georgia Tech library contains over 1.9 million volumes. Together the university libraries of the University System held over 7.8 million volumes while the state universities account for 3.3 million (27%) and the colleges account for over one million volumes (10%). In sum, the library holdings of institutions within the University System are among its most impressive accomplishments.

FACULTIES: The faculty of its thirty-four institutions continues to be a major asset in all considerations of the University System's continuing development. At least 9,426 faculty members (in 1998) engaged in the instructional, research, and service programs of their institutions, and each contributed directly or indirectly to the progress of public higher education in Georgia. The talents,

expertise, and commitments of the University System's faculties signify an area of academic responsibility in which the quest
for self-reliance is most evident. With few exceptions, the public universities of Georgia now have the resources and capabilities to educate, train, and develop the faculty members needed
at all levels of higher education.

The faculties of the University System, considered as groups,
are scholars, scientists, and professional specialists. Their academic fields represent the physical and biological sciences, the
behavioral and social sciences, the humanities and fine arts, and
the diverse professional and applied fields that are essential to
undergraduate, graduate, and professional education. Sixty-nine
percent of the faculty members have an earned doctorate degree
and an additional 6.1 percent hold the highest professional degree
in their respective fields of specialization. Thirty-eight percent
of the faculty members are women, many of whom teach in two-
year colleges where they represent 58.3 percent of the teaching
faculties. Nine percent of the University System's faculty members are African-American members; four out of ten minority
faculty members hold appointments at the public historically
black institutions.

An appreciation of faculty competence and performance may
be gleaned from statistical data gathered routinely. Over half
(56%) of the full-time faculty members have tenure, and at least
54 percent of them hold senior rank as full or associate professors.
Over 3,785 (45.8%) faculty members hold rank at one of the four
research universities where they have met additional standards
imposed by peer review in promotion and tenure decisions. An
additional 1,046 (12.6%) hold rank at one of the two regional universities. Twenty-eight percent of the faculty members hold rank
at a state university and the remaining 1,110 (13.4%) faculty members hold rank within a state or two-year college. At the state
university level 23 percent of the faculty are full professors while
in the state or two-year colleges only 16 percent hold the rank of
full professor.

Over 1,400 research and regional university faculty members
(29%) are full professors while their colleagues serve as associate
professors (36%), assistant professors (32.6%), and instructors
(6.7%). The salaries earned by university faculty are determined,
for the most part, by academic discipline or professional specialty,
faculty rank, length of service, the prestige of institutions granting

their highest degree, and the mission of the institution at which they currently serve. Thus, in 1998 the average full-time faculty salaries were $60,276 at the University of Georgia, $74,852 at Georgia Tech, $59,577 at Georgia State, and $76,902 at the Medical College of Georgia. Average salaries at the regional universities were $45,909; at the state universities $47,143; at the state colleges $43,319; and for the two-year colleges $40,714 was the average salary received by their 918 faculty members.

In addition to their faculties, the 34 institutions within the University System employed 2,897 executives or administrators, 7,358 professionals without faculty rank, 5,488 secretaries or clerical workers, 3,545 teaching paraprofessionals, 1,458 skilled-crafts personnel, and 4,126 service or maintenance staff personnel. Altogether, 33,126 individuals were employees of 34 separate institutions "governed, controlled, and managed" by the Board of Regents.

All such statistical data indicate remarkable changes in the faculties of Georgia's public universities and colleges since the severe faculty shortage of the 1960s. Post-WWII faculties who were hastily recruited to teach returning veterans were often replaced by many of their own students, and throughout the 1980s many veterans were replaced by students they had taught in the 1960s. Faculty development policies of "grow your own" had been successful and neither the University System nor the private colleges of Georgia would be overly dependent upon other states or regions for faculty and professional staffs in the years ahead.

STUDENTS: The number and diversity of students, in 1998, make a striking contrast with the 8,035 students enrolled in 1933. In the fall of 1990 the students enrolled in units of the University System were still predominantly white (80.2%) but an increasing number of them (15.7%) were African American and an appreciable number of enrolled students (4.1 %) were members of other racial or ethnic groups. Except for the universities where over half (51.1%) are men, the majority of students in the University System are women (54.9%) and many of them are enrolled on a part-time basis (36.3%). As undergraduates, students in 1990 were older—with an average age of 23.2 years—and in the public two-year colleges the typical student was almost 25 years old.

As the decade of the 1990s closed, the advantages and benefits of Governor Zell Miller's and Chancellor Stephen Portch's concerted leadership were increasingly evident. No less than 200,210 students were enrolled in the University System's 34 institutions of higher education—an enrollment that contrasts sharply with the 8,035 students enrolled in 1933, the 22,651 students enrolled in 1946, the 44,552 enrolled in 1964, and the 105,424 students in 1971 (when the first six-figure enrollment was recorded). The four research universities had a combined enrollment of 69,171 student and the 13 two-year colleges had an enrollment of 36,585 student— a figure exceeding the University System's total enrollment as recent as 1962. The combined enrollments of state universities (64,530) exceeded the University System's total enrollment as recent as 1966, the third year in which "baby-boomers" arrived on college campuses.

The great majority of students (82.4%) were still enrolled in undergraduate programs, but a substantial increase in graduate enrollments was displayed by 27,197 students who represented 13.6 percent of the system's total enrollment. When compared to the state's increased population since 1930, student enrollments are less dramatic but nonetheless indicative of the University System's remarkable growth. In 1933 the ratio of students (8,035) to population (2.9 million) was .0025 and suggests that for every ten thousand Georgians, 25 students were enrolled in a unit of the University System. In 1998 the ratio of students to population (7.1 million) was .0281 and suggested an attendance of 281 students for every ten thousand Georgians. Thus, the impressive and continuing increases in student enrollments since 1933 are indicative of the University System's effectiveness in meeting the educational needs of Georgia citizens and residents.

The abilities and achievement of entering freshmen continue to be indicative of the changing demands and challenges to which all institutions of higher learning must respond. In 1989 the average SAT-Verbal score recorded for entering University System freshmen was 417 and the average SAT-Mathematics score was 455. When interpreted as an index of verbal and mathematical abilities related to effective learning in college courses, SAT scores convey useful and valuable information about the readiness of entering students for the intellectual and academic challenges of college instruction. The average SAT scores of students entering Georgia Tech, Georgia State, and the University of Georgia, thus interpreted, suggest appreciable preparation for college and predictable success in meeting course requirements and instructor expectations. The average scores recorded for students in state and two-year colleges suggest a lesser degree of verbal and mathematical ability but at least half of the students entering such institutions should not have undue difficulty in meeting academic standards.

A similar interpretation of educational achievement can be made from the high school grades reported for entering University System freshmen. In 1989 the mean high school average for entering freshmen was 2.6 (on a 4.0 scale), a level of academic performance that would be regarded as typical or average in most high schools. Averages are misleading, however, and a better interpretation of student abilities and achievement can be made from the distribution of SAT scores and high school grades. In the fall of 1989 less than 12 percent of the entering freshmen came with "A" or "B+" averages in high school; over 16 percent entered with high school grades averaging "D" or lower. The remaining 72 percent, of course, had earned high school averages in the middle range of the grade distribution.

The distribution of SAT scores for University System students discloses three distinct levels of verbal and mathematical ability. In 1989 less than 5 percent (4.1%) of the University System's entering freshmen scored above 600 on the SAT-Verbal scale. Almost exactly half (50.5%) scored in the mid-range between 400 and 600, and 45.2 percent (12,188 students) scored below 400. On the SAT-Mathematics scale 11.7 percent scored above 600 while 55.4 percent scored between 400 and 600 and 33.0 percent scored below 400 points.

Student scores on the two scales suggest better preparation in mathematics than in verbal reasoning, vocabulary, and reading comprehension. Such an interpretation is attenuated, however, by recognition that half of the students (48%) with high SAT-Mathematics scores were at Georgia Tech where admission policies emphasized mathematical ability. This alone could account for the differences in scores above 600 and the average differences between SAT-Verbal and SAT-Mathematics scores.

If SAT-Verbal scores are accepted as the most easily obtained indication of how well entering students will perform in English, history, political science, sociology, and other first-year courses requiring extensive reading, the distribution of SAT-Verbal scores suggests that well prepared freshmen are far out-numbered by poorly prepared freshmen. Less than 5 percent of the 1989 entering students scored 600 or higher on the verbal section of the SAT. Given the admission of 12,188 students who scored below 400 on the SAT-Verbal scale, the enrollment in developmental studies of 19,729 students (11.4% of the total system enrollment) followed as a logical consequence of inadequate high school preparation. The abilities and achievement of entering students thus imply that the excellence of the University System, as a statewide system of public higher education, is limited by the quality of education in the public schools. Commendable progress had been made in establishing a college preparatory curriculum, but in the early 1990s three out of every ten freshmen had not completed a preparatory program of study. In the first three years of addi-tional curricular requirements for admission, the effectiveness of the college preparatory curriculum was not demonstrated by rates of completion or by prevention of placement in develop-mental studies. The program was effective, nonetheless, in iden-tifying more quickly the academic deficiencies of students and in facilitating their exit from developmental studies (*Hudson and Pounds, 1991*).

The assessment of student abilities and achievement at higher levels is implied by the Regents Test (for sophomores) and exit examinations (for seniors). The passing rates for sophomores more or less confirm the reading and writing difficulties of beginning students, but the systemwide passing rate of 73.1 percent in 1998 still does not convey adequate information about students and their basic academic competencies. Institutional passing rates ranging from 28.5 percent to 88.2 percent tell more about problems in dealing with unprepared students than about institutional effectiveness in teaching basic skills of literacy. Thus, variations in student abilities and institutional policies, programs, and ser-vices imply that the assessment of educational outcomes in the form of academic competencies, general achievement, or advanced learning skills remains a major challenge for both the University System and its institutions.

ACADEMIC PROGRAMS: The range and diversity of curricula within the University System are further testament to its effectiveness in responding to changing demands and expectations. Vestiges of a traditional curriculum are apparent in core curriculum require-ments for the humanities, natural sciences, and mathematics but the substance and content of undergraduate courses have changed significantly since the 1950s. Most baccalaureate programs consist of general education courses in the freshmen and sophomore years, with advanced or specialized coursework in the junior and senior years, but many bachelor's degrees now take five years for completion.

The great diversity of program and course offerings are depicted in college catalogs, by the majors declared by students, and by the degrees conferred by institutions. The Bachelor of Arts degree and the Bachelor of Science degree remain the most frequently awarded degrees, but the areas of specialization are innumerable. For the University System, twelve broadly grouped areas of specialization encompass the declared majors of 72 percent of the students. The fields in which students declare majors are: agriculture, business, computer science, education, engineering (or engineering technology), foreign languages, humanities and fine arts, mathematics, nursing, allied health specialties, life sciences, physical sciences, and social sciences. Computer science, engineering technology, and allied health specialties are the most conspicuous additions to the curriculum since the 1950s. Business (21.6%), education (15.7%), engineering/engineering technology (8.5%), and social sciences (7.6%) are the most frequent disciplines in which degrees are conferred. Traditional major fields in foreign languages, mathematics, and physical sciences accounted for less than one percent each in the 21,069 degrees conferred in 1998. Architecture, philosophy, and religion are also fields in which degrees conferred upon less than one percent each of University System graduates, but one percent of over 21,069 graduating seniors amounts to at least 210 graduates.

The number of degrees conferred in areas of specialization by the different levels of institutions also indicates, to an appreciable degree, student demand *and* institutional productivity. In 1998 the four research universities conferred 16,411 degrees, the regional universities conferred 4,444 degrees, the state universities awarded 11,413 degrees, and the two-year colleges conferred 4,140 associate degrees. The total for such degrees was 36,438 degrees.

In Summary the 34 institutions of the University System offer a comprehensive and commendable array of academic degrees, programs, and courses to serve the educational needs and interests of students. Business, education, engineering, and the social sciences are the preferred areas of advanced or specialized education, and the frequency of declared majors and conferred degrees in such fields is indicative of the practical learning needs

and interests that characterize American higher education. The
arts, sciences, and humanities are represented well in the degree
programs of public universities and colleges, but they are chosen
(as major fields of study) by a minority of the system's upper-
division and graduate students.

Institutional Commitments and Contributions

Curricular offerings of public research universities, state
universities, state colleges and two-year colleges are their major
assets and their primary reason-for-being. Numerous other programs, services, and activities are needed, however, for fair-and-
equitable use by other Georgia citizens and residents. During
the years 1966-1976 when undergraduate education was subjected
to rapid change, the institutions of the University System were
spared some of the ineffective curricular revisions that were
masked as innovative reforms. On many occasions institutional
and systemwide leadership, status, and policies acted as a much
needed flywheel. Within the 34 institutions of the University
System, as elsewhere, significant changes are yet to be fully
assimilated and there are many ways in which undergraduate
teaching *and* learning could be improved. Arbitrary program
standards, course requirements, and instructor expectations persist, but the development of other programs and services are
responsive to the changing needs and demands of the University
System's many constituencies. Thus the University System occu-
pies a more favorable position from which to plan and develop
effectively the academic programs and services needed to meet
changing demands and expectations in the 21st century.

PUBLIC SERVICE AND RESEARCH: Institutional commitments to public
service are clearly seen in the numerous continuing education,
in-service training, short-term instruction, and professional
development programs for citizens and residents who are not
formally enrolled as students in any of the major public universities, state universities, or two-year colleges. Commitment and
effectiveness are further demonstrated in the various functions
and activities of the Georgia Center for Continuing Education
(UGA), the Cooperative Extension Service (UGA), the Institute
of Higher Education (UGA), the Rural Development Center
(Tifton), the Economic Development Laboratory (GT), and the
Urban Life Center (GSU). The nature and extent of its many

services to state, county, or municipal government and to local communities are evident in the work of Institute of Government (UGA), the Economic Forecasting Center (GSU), and various other institutes or centers with missions related to the state's social, economic, political, and technological development.

In addition to many institutes and centers with explicit responsibilities for working with the University System's public constituencies, numerous programs, projects, and activities are sponsored and conducted by USGA institutions and their various divisions. In 1998 at least 21,250 programs, involving over 380,000 participants, were planned, organized, and conducted by units of the system's 34 institutions. The productivity of such public service programs is evident from the generation of over 484,000 continuing education units (CEU's). Almost thirty percent of these programs were by the six major universities; over four out of ten (40.9%) were conducted by the state universities and the remaining 29.4 percent was conducted by the state and two-year colleges. The extent and variety of such programs reflect a commendable response to public expectations of the state's colleges and universities as an available source of personal, social, professional, and technical assistance.

The magnitude of research responsibilities is shown by the contracts and grants expenditure of over $536.7 million in 1998. The University of Georgia expended over $483.2 million in research funds, while Georgia Tech spent at least $187.1 million. Georgia State spent $61.0 million and the Medical College spent $102.4 million. Distinctive research facilities and programs for the University of Georgia are the Complex Carbohydrate Research Center, the Computational Quantum Chemistry Center, the Savannah River Ecology Laboratory, the Marine Institute on Sapelo Island, the Skidaway Institute of Oceanography, and the agricultural experimental stations—with three main stations at Griffin, Tifton, and Athens, and five branch stations at Blairsville, Calhoun, Eatonton, Midville, and Plains.

Distinctive facilities and programs for Georgia Tech are the Georgia Tech Research Institute, which consists of seven major research laboratories, the Microelectronics Research Center, the Health Systems Research Center, and the Technology Policy and Assessment Center. Georgia State conducts most of its research within its colleges of Arts and Sciences, Business, Health Sciences, Public and Urban Affairs, and Education but may boast of its

Language Research Center and its Economic Forecasting Center, its Economic Policy Center, and its Center for High Angular Resolution Astronomy. The Medical College can take pride in the Alzheimers Basic and Clinical Research Center, the Comprehensive Sickle Cell Center, the Georgia Institute of Human Nutrition, and the Georgia Institute for Prevention of Human Disease and Accidents.

National rankings of Georgia Tech, Georgia State, the Medical College and the University of Georgia reflect their increasing national recognition as research universities. The range and diversity of research within the System's universities is impressive and the remarkable progress made since the mid-1960s underscores the increasing public investment in Georgia's institutions of higher education.

LOOKING BACK, it is obvious that the institutions of the University System are well distributed geographically to meet their various commitments and to make their specific contributions demographically accessible as well as geographically available. In other words, more programs and services should be within the reach of people who live in heavily concentrated areas, as well as those who live in isolated rural areas of the State. The geographical proximity of other institutions should not influence unduly the establishment of extension centers, resident graduate centers, and new institutions when the adult learner population warrants additional or other kinds of educational opportunities.

Institutional policies and programs have dealt with the issue of unprepared students in at least five notable efforts. One of the reasons for adopting the SAT was to identify students needing academic assistance. Later a college preparatory curriculum was adopted to strengthen secondary preparation in English, mathematics, and science. Developmental studies programs were mandated as a concerted effort to remedy academic deficiencies and a college placement exam was developed to facilitate placement in courses appropriate for the different levels of student achievement. And a systemwide test of basic skills has been required to ensure standards of academic competence in transferring to upper division coursework. The University System's efforts in all five programs has been instructive and beneficial, but the challenge of teaching basic skills to educationally disadvantaged students remains a "recurring issue" in public higher education.

The provision of general education to students interested in advanced, specialized, or technical programs is a challenge as old as that of assisting unprepared students. Virtually all critics of higher education deplore excessive specialization and advocate a broader diffusion of general knowledge and information to college graduates. Graduate schools, employers, and society at large, however, tend strongly to recognize those who specialize in technical or advanced fields of knowledge. The University System's core curriculum assures that students will take courses in English, mathematics, history, and science but the benefits of a general or liberal education still escape far too many college graduates. The prominence of business, education, engineering, and social science in declaring majors and earning degrees is of a continuing challenge and/or issue in undergraduate education.

The challenge of curricular revision is obscured by the gradual, incremental changes that take place continuously in course content and substance. Undergraduate curricula, in particular, are changed as course requirements and faculty expectations are altered through daily lectures and class discussions. As a result, the guidance and direction of curricular change can become an issue at all levels of academic governance. And indeed, the most cumbersome process in higher education may be the review and approval of proposals for new courses and degree programs. Quite often the name of a division, school, or college will not be changed until long after its curriculum has undergone gradual but nonetheless profound changes. Not until 1991 did the University of Georgia's College of Agriculture become the College of Agricultural and Environmental Sciences; the College of Home Economics became the College of Family and Consumer Sciences only one year earlier.

Business, education, engineering, technology, and health care remain areas of specialization in which curricular planning and development are particularly relevant. Pressures for curricular change are intense because each field of specialization is influenced significantly by changing public demands and technological innovations. The arts, sciences, and humanities are under similar pressure to "internationalize" undergraduate curricula by giving better coverage to other societies and cultures. Other conditions fostering planned-and-directed change in college and university curricula are international competition in a global economy, and the acceleration of technological and sociocultural change in international relations. All things considered, the guidance and direction of curricular change may be one of the University System's persistent challenges in the 21st century.

The continuing contributions of innumerable individuals within the University System's institutions are another valuable but often intangible resource. Among the faculties, staffs, alumni, and benefactors of the various institutions are many individuals who serve public higher education well. Alumni, in particular, promote the best interests of their respective institutions and make many valuable contributions. Many faculty members teach, research, and serve well without dissent or fanfare. And staff members of all institutions serve in many effective ways as intermediaries for students and other clients.

At their worst, community pride and boosterism reflect institutional aspirations that do not always serve the University System well. At their best, community pride and support give colleges and universities another perspective on institutional mission and serve, on many occasions, as a buffer against forms of adversity that do not reach the rooms of governing boards. The vitality and effectiveness of institutions, programs, and services are often influenced in unpublicized but meaningful ways. Such influences are only partially evident in community service programs or in the enthusiasm that comes with national championships in intercollegiate athletics. As an intangible resource, community investments in local institutions serve in many different ways to foster in the long run a climate for educational, intellectual, and cultural advancement.

As the historical development of its institutions so clearly demonstrate, the responsiveness of the University System to public needs, demands, and expectations is essential to their mutual missions and roles in state and society. As a statewide system of public higher education, the University System continues to serve well its many constituencies and its state, region, and nation. The personnel, programs, services, and activities of thirty-four relatively diverse institutions have contributed significantly and substantially to the state's social, economic, and political development. Public perceptions and expectations of the institutions have changed as their larger, more significant role in the state and region's economic, technological, and cultural advancement have continued to grow and develop.

Chapter Eight
Continuing Progress and Maturity: 1994-2001

The University System of Georgia will hold itself accountable to the citizens of Georgia for the effective and efficient use of every available resource, new technology, . . . human insight and activity to achieve access to academic excellence for all citizens and to charge its collective intellectual power on behalf of the state.

A Vision For The University System
January 12, 2000

In 1999 the state of Georgia was identified in a national study as "the beneficiary of a strong economy and a sup portive governor." The University System was identified as "a unified system of higher education with constitutional authority." As the nation's tenth most populous state, Georgia could take pride in its commitments to public higher education. To be chosen for a national study including California, New York, Michigan, Illinois, Texas, and Florida is a compliment that is clearly indicative of the University System's continuing progress and its maturity as a unified statewide system of public higher education.

The University System's continued development and improvement has been evident in its progress for well over a half-century. The growth patterns of the past can be depicted as six distinct periods of growth and development that signify substantive and enduring change. In each period of growth (or stage of development) the University System had become *one* assemblage of institutions, personnel, programs, and services in the beginning and was becoming *another* in the end. In each stage of development the University System encountered adversities that delayed the advantages and benefits of higher education for numerous Georgia residents and citizens. And in each stage, with minor exceptions, progress was marked by increased enrollments, better programs, extended services, and increasingly competent personnel. Setbacks have indeed been a part of each stage of development but growth, progress, and improvement have been observable throughout the University System's history.

In retrospect, 1932-1950 were years of trial-and-error in which there were few guiding precedents for developing with severely limited resources a statewide system of higher education. Growth of the new University System was also hampered by deep-seated convictions that Georgia was a poor state and would remain a poor state. Nonetheless there was an increasing awareness of the value of higher education in the state's social, economic, and political advancement. Despite poverty, political interference, loss of accreditation, and World War II the University System benefited substantially from federal assistance in buildings and programs—and from the Works and Strayer reports that defined educational liabilities and deficits.

The years 1950-1964 began with reasons for despair and closed with an optimistic outlook that the University System had not known previously. Anti-intellectualism, a reactionary political climate, and uncertain economic growth in the early 1950s gave no indication of the "growth psychology" that characterized the 1960s. The prospects for federal assistance, the removal of deseg-regation shackles, the arrival on campus of baby boomers, and the enthusiasm of the space age were contributing factors nation-ally and regionally. Equally significant was a new and different attitude toward higher education and its role in the development of human capital.

A brief growth period 1964-1972 encompasses nine years of the University System's most interesting growth *and* at least five of its most difficult years. The establishment of new colleges, the development of new programs, and the recruitment of new faculties proceeded at a pace that no one had anticipated. The "massive" federal funding of the 1960s and a "break-through" in state funding in 1968 were part of a floodtide that reached rocky shores almost immediately. In that brief period, however, the University System enrolled an average 8,028 additional students each year and grew at an annual rate of 18 percent.

The financial crisis of the early 1970s found the University System with many added responsibilities and its only serious loss of public confidence. Public policy dictated the centraliza-tion of numerous institutional policy decisions as the federal government placed a firm emphasis on institutional planning, management, and evaluation. National enrollment projections depicted a future in which traditional college-age students (18-22 years) would be a minority, and virtually all national conferences included at least one session on nontraditional students and/or adult learners. Thus the years of 1972-1984 were a growth period in which the financial exigencies of higher education dictated an inordinate concern with accountability, managerial efficiency, cost-effectiveness, and other concepts (or models) borrowed from the nation's business corporations. Unfortunately for institutions of public higher education, national objectives and priorities encouraged hastily planned programs of study for a new generation of students. One noted outcome of the effort was an erosion of academic standards on many college campuses.

The University System's fifth growth period 1984-1990 witnessed a rapid turnover in institutional leadership, a loosening of centralized control, and a re-emergence of institutional aspirations. Changes in leadership brought changes in administrative styles *and* the commitments of institutional leaders to previous plans, policies and practices. Enrollments expanded in unprecedented ways, and institutional missions changed with or without deliberate planning and policy decisions. A noticeable characteristic of the late 1980s was the unevenness with which the institutions of the University System grew and developed. Like sectors of the national economy, institutions with fortunate growth patterns fared well while institutions with disadvantages were disadvantaged further.

Embedded in the University System's growth patterns were many irregular, uneven, and unexpected developments. No observer, critical or uncritical, would contend that the University System of Georgia was the work of a master planner or the result of grand design. A crucial factor, therefore, is the absence of any period in which there were sustained efforts to retrench or to control growth and expansion across institutions and across programs. There have been years in which financial support was reduced temporarily and a slower growth rate was evident, but reductions in financial support have usually been a function of state revenues and not deliberate policy decisions.

Much of the University System's growth is related, of course, to growth in the state of Georgia's population and economy. In

1930, as mentioned previously, the population of Georgia was less than three million people and until 1960 when the population had grown to almost four million, the state's growth in population was seldom a factor in educational thought and discussion. Having taken many decades to reach 3.9 million, Georgia's population gained an additional 2.5 million in the next thirty years. The growth of the state's economy is seen in similar statistics. As *per capita* income has increased and approached the national average, so have state appropriations for higher education.

Unfortunately, the University System's budget was significantly reduced in 1990 and 1991 as the result of a lingering recession in the state's economy. Once again the University System had entered a "stage of development" with expectations that were suddenly altered. And once again public perceptions of the University System's needs were at variance with public demands for its programs and services. The University System's resources, capabilities, and expertise were essential to the state's economic, technological, and cultural advancement but improvement of institutions, facilities, programs, and services were not a priority in years of declining state revenues.

The University System's sixth, most recent, and most impressive growth period encompasses six years of Governor Zell Miller's executive leadership and seven years of Chancellor Stephen Portch's outstanding commitment in bringing the University System to a higher level of national visability and recognition. Thus, the years **1994-2001** can be bracketed as the years in which the University System of Georgia became the nation's fourth largest statewide system of public higher education.

Georgia, as the nation's tenth most populous state, could not be listed as one of the nine "mega-states" in which over half of the nation's population lived. It could claim, however, to be the largest of the nation's forty-one "smaller states." The fortuitous conditions under which the University System achieved its national status were readily acknowledged. In addition to the advantages and benefits of a progressive governor and an enthusiastic chancellor, the University System was well served by the state's growth and robust economy, the international attraction of Atlanta as the site of the 1996 Summer Olympics, the cooperative assistance of the state legislature, and the full commitment of the Board of Regents.

Also relevant to the University System's continuing progress and maturity was the technological revolution in communications and the electronic transfer of data, information, and knowledge with their many implications for intellectual and cultural advancement. Within its 34 institutions and throughout the University System, innovative and rapid changes were taking place and thereby opening many unanticipated opportunities and interesting challenges. And if the state is not literally the "campus" of the University System, its units are actively involved in all geographic areas of Georgia. In its own right and much to its own credit, the University System continues to be a growing, developing, and maturing institution that had learned much from its experiences in a state that changed dramatically during the 20th century.

Systemwide Planning for a Statewide System

Beginning in 1994 with their vision statement of what the University System could be—and a useful list of "guiding principles"—the Regents launched a planning process that challenged the Regents, Chancellor Portch and his staff, and administrative leaders in thirty-four institutions to write their own mission statements, to set goals and priorities, and to work together for the benefit of the University System as a unified whole.

The ground rules for *envisioning* were well specified. In their respective categories—as research, regional, or state universities, and state or two-year colleges—each institution developed its mission statement "within the context of the University System's mission and vision" and with respect to the "core characteristics" it shared with similarly classified institutions. Having embodied these common characteristics, each institution then took into account variations in its purposes, histories, traditions, and settings, and thereby focused on its own distinctiveness and accomplishments.

In such ways, a commendable logic was brought to the numerous changes in institutional names during the 1990s. More important, no doubt, was the defining of institutional missions in a manner that identified the role and responsibilities of each university or college as a unit within a statewide system of public higher education. The commitments and the contributions of each institution thus would be both general and specific, with each having a distinctive role to play in a larger and more significant endeavor.

Organization and Governance

The Regents, much to their credit, defined *their mission* in the beginning. They were committed to raising the educational level of Georgia citizens and residents, to improving the quality of education at all levels, to providing basic and applied research, as well as public service, to the University System's many constituencies—and to the state and society in which they lived.

As the Board of Regents' operational staff, the Office of the Chancellor remained committed to the University System of Georgia, the board and their 34 institutions, the state of Georgia, and other constituencies. The mission, role, and responsibilities of *The Chancellor's Office and Staff* are stated as follows:

- promote a perspective on higher education that would attend to the current and developing needs of the state;
- provide leadership in analyzing, monitoring, and interpreting trends and developments;
- provide assistance in all phases of strategic planning;
- guide institutions in implementing Regents policies and procedures;
- foster strong relationships, open communications, and collaboration among the system's institutions;
- act as stewards of the state's higher education resources;
- set the highest standards for educational policy and practices, promote collaboration with other agencies in public and private sectors (especially the public schools and technical colleges);
- link the University System with business, government, and communities to encourage economic development (by increasing the state's intellectual capital); and by no means the least of responsibilities:
- develop, propose, and promote the University System budget request to the General Assembly.

As the duties and responsibilities of the Office of the Chancellor change in meeting the challenges of its mission, so do the competencies, assignments, and size of the chancellor's professional staff. If at any time in the past, the efficiency or effectiveness of the chancellor's staff were judged by its small size and thrifty payroll, assistant vice chancellors of the past would be astounded by the size and composition of the University

System's administrative staff in the year 2002. They would also be amazed at the facilities of "the Central Offices" and the resources at the staff's disposal.

The organizational chart of the Board of Regents *(2001)* displays three senior vice chancellors reporting to the chancellor who, of course, is the only person reporting directly the Regents. Also reporting directly to the chancellor was the president and CEO of Georgia GLOBE, a unit established for "Global Learning Online for Business and Education:

Reporting to the Senior Vice Chancellor for *Academic and Fiscal Affairs* are three vice chancellors and an associate vice chancellor who are responsible for (1) academic, faculty, and student affairs, (2) fiscal affairs, (3) information and instructional technology, and (4) strategic research and analysis, respectively. Reporting to the vice chancellors are two other associate vice chancellors and five assistant vice chancellors, each with responsibilities related to academic affairs such as faculty relations, testing, planning, student services, newly acquired responsibilities identified as advanced learning technologies, cooperative relations with elementary and secondary education, and library services.

Reporting to the Senior Vice Chancellor for *External Affairs and Facilities* are two vice chancellors appropriately identified with the two functions for which their senior vice chancellor is responsible. Two assistant vice chancellors are in charge of "media and publications" or "development—economic services". Two assistant vice chancellors (design & construction; facilities) and two directors (environmental safety; planning) report directly to the vice chancellor for facilities.

The Senior Vice Chancellor for *Support Services* oversees the responsibilities of two associate vice chancellors, one for human resources and the other for legal affairs—and one assistant vice chancellor who is identified with internal auditing. Two assistant vice chancellors report to the associate vice chancellor for legal affairs in carrying out their duties, as related to "legal affairs/contracts and legal affairs/prevention".

All such organizational charts are subject to change, no doubt, with or without advanced notice. Note should be taken, however, that at least twenty-nine professional staff members were identified (in 2001) as senior, associate, or assistant vice chancellors. In many respects, a similar "filling of the administrative ranks" may be observed on university campuses where senior, associate, and assistant vice presidents are assigned similar duties and responsibilities.

The accomplishments of the University System, as a statewide system, are clearly evident in the diversification of its institutions: four research universities, two regional universities, thirteen state universities, plus thirteen state colleges and two two-year colleges. Within the 34 institutions comprehensive programs of study are offered in professional, general, special, technological, practical, and traditional fields of education. The faculties are actively engaged in the instruction of students—and professional, scientific, and scholarly inquiry into the social, economic, technological, and cultural issues that concern the state, nation, and world environment in which Georgians live.

The presidents of University System institutions are appointed upon recommendation of the chancellor—and may be re-assigned or dismissed upon the chancellor's recommendation. Presidents of the thirty-four institutions are thereby the major link by which the authority and responsibilities of the Board of Regents are conveyed to relatively autonomous institutions located at varying distances from the University System's central offices.

Many Georgians continue to believe that appointment to the Board of Regents is the most prestigious of all honors to be bestowed in state government. As a constitutional body, the Board of Regents cooperate with the governor and the General Assembly in matters pertaining to annual appropriations and budgets, but the board maintains discretionary authority in allocation of state funds to the separate 34 institutions of higher learning. The chancellor, serving at the pleasure of the Board of Regents, continues to oversee all matters pertaining to the funding of public universities and colleges, their administration, and their operations. In the public's eyes, the chancellor continues to be the state's most prestigious official as well as the highest ranking administrator in higher education.

In retrospect, systemwide planning in the 1990s was no longer anathema to institutional aspirations and systematic planning was no longer a periodic initiative by progressive governors. Indeed, the continuing development of the state's universities and colleges had produced a substantial fund of knowledge, resources, and expertise that could be well employed in addressing public policy issues. The leadership of the University System, at all levels, was more amenable to institutional change and the improvement of programs and services. Presidents and other institutional officials also were better informed on national, regional, and state efforts in assessment, accountability, and accreditation. Despite occasional intrusions of "politics" in academic decisions, the University System's progress has been made with appreciable confidence and self-reliance.

Issues, Initiatives and Incentives

When the University System of Georgia's strategic planning *process* is viewed "as a whole" with its own components, constituencies, strategies, goals and priorities, stages or phases, schedules and expected outcomes—it is indeed an impressive and highly significant endeavor by a governing or coordinating board. When all inputs or intakes, outputs or outcomes, and the multi-dimensional features of the process are examined, the advantages and benefits of the overall seven-year effort are surely worthy of praise and emulation.

The commitments and contributions of the University System's many constituencies—governing board members, central office administrators and professional staffs, state officials, public sponsors and benefactors, and public-minded faculties, students, and alumni—are too numerous for detailed appraisal and fairness to all. Nonetheless, the commendable scope and comprehensive reach of the University System's strategic planning process can be documented by the selective citation of the issues addressed, the projects and programs initiated, and the remarkable incentives extended to the University System's participants, constituencies, and beneficiaries throughout the state of Georgia.

Issues: Among the various issues addressed in the University System's strategic planning process were the lingering difficulties of inordinate institutional aspirations, needless program duplication, transfer of credit, remedial courses for poorly prepared students, program transfer (as a means of complying with federal regulations), and admission policies in general.

Other issues were more significant and in retrospect, it is evident that some issues could not be resolved without strong leadership from the Board of Regents, the governor, and the

General Assembly. Among these issues were cooperative relations between the University System, the public schools within the state, and the technical schools under the control of the Department of Technical and Adult Education, The changing climate of public opinion and the changing needs and demands of the public for postsecondary education required policy decisions at a higher level than the local community.

Some issues were addressed and ameliorated with the reclassification of senior colleges as state universities, the development of less ambitious mission statements by institutions previously perceiving other institutions as competitors *and* not as units of the same University System. Indeed, the most significant and meaningful feature of the overall planning process was the directive that institutional missions must be in keeping with system-wide policies, goals, and priorities of the University System in its commitments to "ensure access to excellence and educational opportunity" as a unified statewide system of public higher education. Thereby institutional aspirations were curbed by missions, goals, and priorities that were not competitive with other units of the same system.

Admission policies could be developed at four distinct levels of entry determined by the distinctive missions of research, regional, and state universities, and two year colleges. Care was taken to phase in, with advance notice, changes that could be perceived as too radical for reluctant constituencies. Despite the most enlightened policies imaginable, admission standards and noncredit courses for the improvement of basic skills are recurrent sources of disagreement on many college campuses. As learning needs and interests change gradually with the admission of each new first-year class, so do faculty interest and standards change incrementally with appointments and retirements.

Initiatives: The wisdom of viewing the University System as a unified system and the strategic effectiveness of the overall planning process can be seen in initiatives taken at the system level and their statewide effect on public higher education. By obtaining the necessary funding for innovative projects, the University System could directly address and accomplish educational goals and objectives in keeping with state priorities. Lifelong observers of social, economic, political, or educational scenes in Georgia would be at a loss to suggest a period of seven years in which governors, legislators, chancellors, and governing boards accomplished greater progress or acted more responsively to educational needs beyond the high school.

No single feature tells the story better than the funding of projects to achieve statewide goals and priorities. In a commendable initiative to provide "universal access" to information in the state's public, school, college, and university libraries, GALILEO (a project to create a statewide electronic library system) has been funded annually since 1995—with appropriations ranging from $9.9 million to $3.7 million. By the year 2001, all 34 units of the University System, 35 technical institutes, 40 private institutions, 192 school systems (K-12), 58 public library systems, and various state agencies, such as the governor's office and legislative research offices, had access to GALILEO resources. At that time "lifetime usage statistics" exceeded 34.2 million logins to various databases. Another initiative, related to GALILEO, provided access to "digital" records of Georgia's cultural and historical resources.

Other projects, extending the advantages and benefits of information technology to education, assisted classroom teachers in their efforts to use more effectively the technological innovations at their disposal, assisted students in using information technology for individualized instruction, and in the provision of innovative services to students and teachers, as individuals in each group pursued nontraditional goals and objectives by nonconventional methods and means.

Among the impressive initiatives dealing with online learning, the University System has provided "distance learning" since the year 2000 through Georgia GLOBE (an apt acronym for Global Learning Online for Business and Education). Two years later Georgia GLOBE provided academic credit for almost 500 distance learning opportunities in addition to its continuing education and/or professional development courses. Online by that time was a ten-course graduate program leading to a Master of Business Administration (MBA) degree. In such efforts GLOBE worked closely with the Southern Regional Education Board's Electronic Campus and thereby gave Georgians access to as many as 5,000 online courses and 250 degree programs and involving over 300 colleges and universities.

In 2001 over 40,000 students were engaged in distance learning, by means related to Georgia GLOBE, with the master's degree in business as their "most popular" choice. At the elementary and secondary levels of education, readiness and enrichment programs reached out to middle school children and high school students in concerted efforts to established better working relationships with future applicants to the state's public, private, and/ or technical colleges. Other initiatives addressed the preparation of Georgia school teachers, facilitated the contacts of prospective employers with employable graduates, advised students on the availability of academic programs and careers, directed newcomers to student services and opportunities, and sought, in general, to create an academic environment in which students were better informed about academic possibilities and opportunities.

In similar manner, other initiatives addressed the advantages of instructional technology in the improvement and effectiveness of both teaching and learning at all levels: undergraduate, professional, and graduate. Of special note at this point is the emphasis given the development of a "Statewide Desktop Learning Network" to meet degree, credit, and noncredit needs of Georgia citizens. At the same time, the roots of our academic heritage was nourished by a special initiative that defined the mission of Georgia College & State University as Georgia's public liberal arts college. In fulfilling its mission, GC&SU will maintain a lower student/faculty ratio and provide a liberal education consistent with that of similar institutions nationally.

Other efforts to acknowledge and conserve the intellectual and cultural heritage of the University System and its institutions are evident in: (a) initiatives protecting public investments, financial and otherwise, *and* (b) in USGA facilities and their renovation as well as their modernization and repair. The initiative to enhance the resources and capabilities of Fort Valley State, Savannah State, and Albany State Universities and to fully recognize their distinctive commitments and contributions was especially appropriate. This initiative not only enhanced the image of three distinctive institutions, but the University System of Georgia as well.

Perhaps the most daring or ambitious initiative of the University System's strategic plan is ICAPP: Georgia's Intellectual Capital Partnership Program. Funded annually since 1997 with an average of $4.60 million, ICAPP seeks improvement in the state's economic development by attracting "high-quality jobs" and "strategic new industry"; preparing Georgians as "knowledge workers"; and developing active partnerships with business and industry, government, cultural and social organizations. The intent thereby is to analyze, project, and respond to state and regional needs.

To a certain extent, ICAPP may be viewed as a strategically effective use of University System institutions, resources, capabilities, and expertise in regional development within the state. Many features of the project are quite promising and in years to come, ICAPP may be regarded as the most successful of all the University System's initiatives in the 1994-2001 era.

Incentives: Considering the scope, magnitude, and complexity of the University System's strategic planning process over a seven-year period, many observers will agree that the most amazing characteristic of the overall process was the incentives given participants and constituencies at various levels and in virtually all areas. With funding for the plan's numerous initiatives, the success of the University System's efforts never seemed in doubt. With the sustained commitments of the governor, the leadership and contributions of the chancellor, the continued support of the General Assembly, and the institutional leadership of presidents and their professional staffs—the active participation, involvement, and commitments of numerous, if not countless, constituencies was assured.

In fiscal year 1996, by directing 18 percent of "new formula budgeting" on a competitive proposal basis, the Regents gave a significant incentive to institutions to develop innovative projects that would increase program efficiency and effectiveness. To encourage collaboration within and without the University System, the Regents funded projects that could raise academic program quality and serve state needs by doing so. In fiscal year 2002, the University System funded "National Patterns of Excellence" programs at Floyd College, the Medical College of Georgia, and the University of Georgia. The total number of awards for "Program Collaboration" was seventeen, with all 34 institutions being involved in one or more collaborative efforts.

Looking back, it is fairly obvious that the University System had much more than a supportive governor and a favorable economy in its favor. No one will deny the importance of Project HOPE in the funding of Initiatives—or the relevance of the "Information Revolution" in stimulating active participation—or various circumstances of the 1990s (nationally, regionally, statewide, and locally) that were unprecedented and unlikely to occur again.

In brief, the University System's strategic planning for "access to academic excellence" stimulated thought, discussion, and action in the advancement of public higher education—and thereby enlisted participants who made commitments and contributions of commendable value to the University System's vision of a "unified whole." Whether judged by its holistic effects or in the remarkable summation of its synergistic parts, the university system had become by the "turn of the century" the state of Georgia's most valuable resource.

Assessment and Accountability

In fiscal year 2002 the budget of the University System exceeded 4.5 billion dollars, more than 217,000 students were enrolled, and at least 35,000 faculty and staff members were employed. The economic impact of thirty-four institutions, their faculties, staffs, and students, was described by the Selig Center for Economic Growth at the University of Georgia as "massive", and the overall effect was reported as generating over 100,000 jobs and infusing eight billion dollars into the communities in which the institutions were located. In any comparison with the social, economic, and cultural costs of an educated citizenry, public higher education in Georgia is not only *big* business, it is public enterprise serving the best interests of state, society, and nation.

Other advantages and benefits of the University System's many programs, services, and activities are too intangible to calculate returns on the investments of state or society. We need not doubt that the state of Georgia is a more attractive place to live and to work because of the University System's development as a comprehensive and unified system of public higher education. Project HOPE, alone, is an acceptable explanation of the state's attractiveness to the immigration of degree-holding parents with school-age children who will later attend college. Numerous other factors and conditions have contributed to the University System's growth. The advantages of time-and-place by having its central offices in Atlanta and across the street from the State Capitol Building quickly come to mind. Other benefits can be identified in the home offices of the Southern Regional Education Board and the Southern Association of Colleges and Schools, the regional offices of the College Board (CEEB) and Educational Testing Service (ETS), and other regional offices that contributed to Atlanta's emergence as a city well suited for national offices. And to an appreciable extent, the challenge to cast off its reputation as a provincial, if not backward, state in the South can be attributed to the increasing emphasis placed on the improvement of its "human resources" throughout the 20th century.

Accountability Reports

In meeting the many challenges encountered in its strategic planning process, the University System has placed a commendable emphasis on public demands and expectations for accountability in meeting strategic goals and state priorities. Given the scope and magnitude of the University System's Special Funding Initiatives, the wisdom of issuing annual accountability reports is readily appreciated. The Regents are indeed mindful of their responsibility to be accountable, and neither the Governor nor the General Assembly have lacked detailed reports on the University System's continuing progress throughout its strategic planning process.

As the seventh annual accountability report (FY2002) discloses, the Regents have continued to advance their mission of ensuring access to academic excellence and educational opportunities. They have "accepted the challenge" and "seized the opportunities" of an ongoing planning process that has created, in turn, other challenges and other opportunities. With modifications-as-needed in their Vision and Mission statements, the Regents have continuously appraised or evaluated the initiatives they have taken and the issues for which they have formulated improved policies. Examples of the "learning" inherent in planning as an ongoing process may be seen in the establishment of "a new technology factor" in the University System's funding base, in the appointment of a new Standing Committee on Information and Instructional Technology, and in defining new strategic goals for "Phase Two" of the University System's Strategic Planning Process.

In holding themselves accountable for the funds and resources expended in taking so many special initiatives, the Regents assumed unprecedented responsibility for achieving systemwide goals and statewide priorities—and showed remarkable courage. Projects such as GALILEO and Georgia GLOBE can be supported dramatically with impressive statistics concerning usage of services, contacts established, and programs or activities of record.

Some projects (e.g. GeorgiaHire) can attest to over 117,000 resumes received by Georgia employers from Georgia students and alumni—and underscore statements such as, "has proven to be a tremendous success." Other projects (P-16 Partnerships) can point to indices such as fifteen local P-16 councils, 29 PREP sites, two gifted academies, and a statewide network to build grassroots support as proof that constructive steps have been taken and favorable results are likely to follow.

In projects dealing with graduate education, regional engineering programs, cooperative doctoral programs, enhancing institutional resources and capabilities, and facilitating access for students overlooked in the past, the demonstration of definite steps taken in the right direction may be sufficient for the time being. In programs for eminent scholars, collaborative research crucial to the health of Georgia citizens, and the fulfillment of special institutional missions, continued progress will often speak for itself. Whenever the general public and their elected representatives know that worthy goals and definite priorities have been identified and progress is being made, accountability can be perceived as an amiable responsibility to keep the public well informed.

State of the System

To an appreciable extent, Chancellor Portch's "State of the System" report in November 2001 may give the best summary of the progress made in the University System's seven years of strategic planning. As the primary participant-observer in the overall process of strategic planning—and as an crucial contributor in all forms of transactional and transformative leadership at state, system, and institutional levels, the chancellor's appraisal of the University System's status and accomplishments in his seven years tenure is worthy of our closest attention. The chancellor clearly indicates that, "The state of the University System of Georgia has never been better." With the largest enrollment and brightest students in its history, the System has never been stronger or bigger.

Among the many indices of increased enrollment, higher SAT scores, better retention rates, and improved standards, the chancellor took special note of new admission requirements that had been successfully implemented—and the encouraging decline in the percent of traditional freshmen who needed assistance in

mastering basic academic skills. In 1995, 27 percent of the freshman class needed assistance; in 2001, 15 percent were required to
seek assistance. With students better prepared *for* college, the
chancellor was confident that they would do better *in* college.

In his report the chancellor acknowledged the benefits of
strong presidential leadership throughout the University System,
the value of differentiated missions for 34 institutions of public
higher education, defining Georgia College & State University
as the state's public liberal arts institution, and reaffirming North
Georgia College & State University's mission as one of four
military colleges in the nation. All USGA institutions were successfully converted to the semester system and all "spoke with
one voice" in the budget process.

Other accomplishments to which he called attention were a
conflict management program and well trained staff members
throughout the system, a recently established Regents' Audit
Committee to continue strong stewardship of public resources,
national recognition of the P-16 and Postsecondary Readiness
Enrichment (PREP) programs, improvements in teacher preparation programs, and references to the ICAPP program as a national
model. In brief, the University System was now recognized nationally for "its innovation, its leadership, and its programs."
Between 1995 and 2000, annual contracts and grants for research
had increased 46 percent and reached a total of $623 million a year.

Also acknowledging that many issues, problems, and challenges
remain, the chancellor identified the state's anti-intellectual cul-
ture, its low rate of participation in postsecondary education, its
need for more financial commitment and innovative thinking, and
the "temporary reduction" in state resources as issues requiring
attention. The gist of his professional (and personal) assessment
of the University System's progress was simple and direct: Georgia now has a strong University System, built on the quality and
hard work of its faculties and staffs, and if not the best system in
the nation, it is deservingly acclaimed as the most improved of
the decade.

Benchmarking and Management Review

In the year 2000 the University System was the subject and
beneficiary of a commendable study conducted by an independent
consulting agency. Five years of strategic planning, financial support, public endorsement, notable achievement, intentional change,

institutional collaboration, and systemwide effort underwent review by professionals without vested interest in the outcomes. The first of two research projects was a benchmarking study in which national peers were identified for the four groups of USGA research universities, regional and state universities, and two-year colleges. Eighteen mission-related criteria/variables were selected by a project steering committee. Thirty-one (bench-marks) or strategic indicators (Input, Process, Output, and Outcome) were agreed upon and data were collected from peer institutions and/or national data sources, as necessary. From the data collected, a normative range was calculated for each of the indicators. If within one standard deviation, above or below the calculated mean of each specific indicator, the indicators for USGA institutions were judged as within, above, or below the normative range of peer institutions.

Using input indicators as an indication of two major dimensions (i.e. quality issues and fiscal issues), the consultants' report points out that most USGA four-year institutions have SAT scores within the normative range established for peer institutions. All two-year colleges received revenues per FTE students *outside* the normative range, and a noticeable number of the USGA institutions were in the normative range for proportion of students in developmental studies. Georgia Tech's SAT scores exceeded those of all peer institutions. Georgia State, the University of Georgia, and the Medical College of Georgia SAT scores fell within the normative range.

With respect to findings from the process indicators, USGA institutions were in the higher level of the normative range on instruction and instruction-related items—a finding that could be attributed to the fact that tenured, full-time faculty members teach a great proportion of undergraduate credit hours. A similar explanation may be in order for the finding that Georgia Tech and seven state universities have administrative expenditures that place them outside the normative range. The recency of revised institutional missions and upgraded classifications may require institutional support to an extent previously unexpected.

In its findings concerning *output* indicators, the consultants' report states that USGA two-year colleges are consistently below the normative range established for peers. When *outcome* indicators are considered, however, they generally demonstrate good results for the system's universities and colleges. General findings concerning the Georgia-Specific Indicators lead to the conclusion that "on the whole" University System institutions perform within the normative range established. "For this," the report states, "the System and its institutions are to be commended".

Of particular note is the finding that lower graduation rates tend to conflict with the Regents' strategic goals to increase the number and quality of USGA graduates. In its goals and priorities, however, for higher admission standards and its initiatives to help K-12 students meet higher standards, the Regents' strategic plan may resolve this particular conflict.

Management Review: The second section of the consultants', report dealt with external and internal performance assessments that would permit recommendations for the improvement of processes for collecting, analyzing, and reporting "data and result." By assessing selected operations at the Regents Central Office and in four institutions representative of research universities (The University of Georgia), state universities (Kennesaw State), state colleges (Macon State), and two-year colleges (Abraham Baldwin), the study identified opportunities for improvement and recommended adoption of "best" practices with institutional and systemwide implication.

Findings and recommendations of the study addressed business services, budgeting procedures, financial reporting, custodial costs, and other institutional processes, as time and opportunity permitted. From these assessments and observations, various recommendations were derived and offered for further study and improvement. Identified, as needing improvement were financial reporting and budget management. Specifically mentioned with praise was the Regents Central Office (for its professional management).

In Summary: The combined results of annual accountability reports, the chancellor's "State of the System" report, and the Benchmarking and Management Report of an independent consulting firm attest to the University System's continuing progress and increasing maturity. The years 1994-2001 have cast spotlights of praise and acclaim on a state at one time experiencing "A Long Dark Night" while the rest of the nation pursued prosperity, if not enlightenment. Thus, it is well to repeat that the progress of the University System from the post WWII years to the beginning of a new century has been gradual—and sometimes hesitant—but progress has been continuous and it has been remarkable. Throughout its years of growth and development, the scope and complexity of education beyond high school have been altered by public demands for broadening, extending, and improving educational opportunities in an open, voluntary society. In meeting its many challenges of changing demands and expectations, the University System has progressed far beyond its early expectations, but it has not yet reached its potential level of growth and development as a unified system of public higher education.

CHAPTER NINE
Continuing Commitment and Leadership: 2001-2002

"Our goal is to be the best in the nation; our curriculum needs to be the best it can be; our faculty and staff needs to be top quality and have the tools and support they need; and our graduates need to be the kind of graduates employers are seeking."

Chancellor Thomas C. Meredith, May 2002

Making his first report to the Board of Regents in January 2002, Chancellor Thomas C. Meredith gave an informed overview of the issues and challenges with which the University System would be dealing in the months ahead. The new chancellor had taken office at a time when state revenues were declining, the state was leading the nation in job losses, and the impact of September 11, 2001 was gaining momentum. He was confronted with a budget that had been cut 2.5 percent in Fiscal Year 2002 and would be cut 5.0 percent in the coming year. Despite "bad economic news" Chancellor Meredith accepted his new responsibilities as challenges that could be met more readily in Georgia than in many other states. The coming year would be "a challenging year" but the University System played a fundamental role in setting the state's agenda, and the Regents had earned an excellent reputation in state government. He added that significant progress had been made, Georgia's promise for the future was bright, and if the University System continued to speak with one voice, it would continue to progress in its efforts to create a more educated Georgia.

Five months later at the State Capitol, the inauguration of the University System's Chancellor, the Governor, the General Assembly, and the Board of Regents reaffirmed in "a historic and colorful ceremony" their commitments to the continued development of public higher education in Georgia. Governor Roy Barnes officially and personally endorsed the chancellor's appointment by stating that the state of Georgia had appointed "the best person possible to lead our great University System." The chancellor responded by assuring the governor that accountability had become the University System's watchword and its economic-development initiatives would be expanded. As chancellor, he pledged that the University System would "lead the way to excellence".

Strategic Goals and System Priorities

In his presentation *(June 2002)* to the Board of Regents, Chancellor Meredith identified the strategic planning goals that would be highlighted in the first year of the Regents' new plan. Goals had been identified in a staff retreat and the focus of strategic planning remained a systemwide response to state needs in providing access and increasing retention rates that would lead to improved graduation rates. The *first* goal addressed the University System's mission of teaching and its efforts to produce graduates who are leaders and contributing citizens.

The *second* and *third* goals, respectively, would increase access by placing programs in locations more accessible to students— and setting new targets for international study abroad programs. Stepped-up efforts to retain students would meet the *fourth* goal by identifying and using "best practices" developed in effective lower division courses. The *fifth* goal would seek ways in which the Intellectual Capital Partnership Program (ICAPP) could be used to predict shortages in human resources and develop strategies to deal with such problems. The University System, as in other statewide systems, would be remiss in its responsibilities if it did not recognize the likelihood of faculty shortages as "baby-boomer" faculty members retire.

The *seventh* and *eighth* goals deal with the funding of facilities and systemic efforts to provide the best facilities possible for students, faculty, and staff. Recognizing that colleges campuses are often "the centerpieces" in the communities they serve, the chancellor emphasized that system facilities should be "constructed with quality materials and maintained properly."

In answering the questions of board members, the chancellor pointed out that many objectives of the previous strategic plan were adjusted in the course of implementation. By presenting the action plan first, he would expect to garner benchmarks as the plan was implemented. As for specific objectives, these were currently being identified and would be added later. As indicated earlier by the chancellor, "several overarching themes" were evident in the overall plan and at least six priorities had been clearly identified. During the next five years, the University System was firmly committed to: (1) a more educated state and a better-prepared society, (2) accountability in funding and the quality of education, (3) being responsive and proactive in meeting state needs, (4) "thinking ahead of the curve" in dealing with expected increases in enrollment, and ensured quality that was paramount, (5) remaining an economic driver in the state's economy, (6) promoting a positive image of the University System, and (7) acting in the state's best interest, thereby maintaining "the posture of moving the state, and not just the system, forward.

Outlook and Prospects

Given the different perspectives of higher education, technical and adult education, and K-12 schooling, the difficulty of keeping an eye of the University System "as a *whole*" is indeed a demanding challenge. In strategic goals concerning partnerships with the State Department of Education and the State Department of Technical and Adult Education, the Regents and the chancellor would meet different kinds of challenge. With a state superintendent of schools elected by Georgia voters and a commissioner of technical and adult education appointed by the governor, the Board of Regents and the chancellor are exposed to the unseemly aspects of local, sub-regional, and state-level politics. Serving at the pleasure of the Board of Regents, the chancellor can plot professional pathways that are less exposed to political crossfire. In return for the shield they provide the chancellor, the Regents can rest assured that the chancellor is not seeking a higher position within the state hierarchy of public offices and honors. In brief, there are compelling reasons for more cooperative efforts between schools, colleges, and universities as part of a much larger, more significant endeavor to develop the state's intellectual capital and enhance human resources that are increasingly needed but seldom plentiful.

All efforts at human capital formation in rapidly changing societies are not as fortunate as Georgia has been in the 1990s and the first two years of the 21st century. As the transition of leadership in the two offices of governor and chancellor certainly

suggested, the state of Georgia continues to benefit from a fortunate combination of circumstances. Future governors and
chancellors are unlikely to have the opportunity and support
that Governor Miller and Chancellor Portch had in the 1990s.
And in all probability, future governors will be unable to contribute with similar effect anything resembling Project HOPE as a
means of providing college scholarships. Even more unlikely in
another era, in another time, is the synergistic effect of an educationally proactive governor, an enthusiastic and articulate
chancellor, a cooperative state legislature, a buoyant, even
prosperous economy, and a climate of public opinion in which
education could be regarded, even if momentarily, as the wisest
investment of public resources.

Other States and Other Systems

To appreciate fully the "emergence" of the University System
of Georgia in the 1990s, it is helpful to look at the differences
between the governance of higher education in Georgia and the
governance, regulation, coordination, or management of higher
education in other states. In doing so the organizational history
of a statewide higher education system should not be insulated
from its political, economic, and/or socio-cultural context. With
all respect to other statewide systems of higher education, it is
difficult to view other systems "as a whole" in the manner that
the Regents strategic planning process views the University System of Georgia. Irrespective of their common responsibilities as
governing, coordinating, regulatory, or consolidated boards,
councils, or commissions, other systems in other states have their
own historical, developmental, and comparative perspectives.

Each state system has its own ties to state government and its
own "experiences" with social, political, economic, and cultural
forces within its state and region. And yet, all recognized state-
level systems are part of a larger national system of postsecondary,
higher, advanced, specialized, and/or professional education. No
federal, state, international or ecumenical body has designed a
national system of higher education, but all constituencies of
state-level systems are affected at one time or another by decisions
or administrative actions taken to comply with the expectations,
demands, or preferences of institutions, associations, or organizations representing national interests.

Through their various "voluntary" associations, institutions of higher education have an advantage over statewide systems in establishing their collective identities and in gaining mutual benefits. The University of Georgia, for example, is readily identified as a land-grant institution by its membership in the National Association of State Universities and Land Grant Colleges (NASULGC). The University System of Georgia was not fully recognized as the nation's fourth largest statewide system of public higher education until the National Center for Public Policy and Higher Education conducted its study of higher education systems in seven of the nation's ten largest states. Entitled, "Designing State Higher Education Systems For a New Century," the DSHES Study provided a wealth of useful information for comparative studies, but all comparisons with institutional peers must be made with caution.

Georgians, in search of favorable comparisons with Michigan, are well advised to consider the constitutional authority of the institutions themselves and the fact that Michigan has no statewide agency with governing responsibilities. It is more difficult, therefore, for fifteen four-year public universities with constitutional authority to view themselves collectively as a "united whole". Comparisons of the University System of Georgia with Illinois' system of higher education will reveal appreciable harmony between "market forces" and institutional autonomy but recognize that the Illinois governor is "given too much power" and the Illinois Board of Higher Education has too little authority. In the 1960s, the University System of Georgia may have envied California for its remarkable Master Plan, its nine campuses for the University of California, and its 22 campuses for California State University. In 2002, however, Georgians will wonder how California's three-segmented "system" continues to educate 1.7 million students and they may question the wisdom of explaining the organization of higher education in California as "a system of subsystems".

In comparisons with the other state higher education systems in the DSHES Study, The Georgia Board of Regents would agree that if the Florida Board of Regents was accurately described as "a corporate board of directors, with the chancellor as its chief executive officer," it would not be inappropriate to look elsewhere for a role model. Just as quickly, perhaps, staff members in the University system's central offices should agree that the demographic, historical, and socio-cultural characteristics of New York and Texas differ significantly and substantially from those of Georgia. They would not see, therefore, a pressing need to emulate the common features or "best practices" of either New York or Texas.

In other words, there is much to learn from comparative studies—especially those using peer groups, benchmarking, etc.—when the object of study is institutions, their constituencies, programs, services, and activities. And there is much to learn from national or regional studies of governing, coordinating, or regulatory state systems of higher education. However, comparative studies of statewide systems, on a one-to-one basis, should be conducted with a healthy, if not stringent, skepticism.

Most of us can learn more about statewide systems of public higher education by studying in more detail our own University System, its institutions, traditions, common features, and specific characteristics. For example, Georgians often forget that the University of Georgia is the nation's first state-chartered state university. In its strategic planning process, the University System of Georgia was wise to make use of comparative data whenever such information is helpful but the quality, efficiency, and effectiveness of its performance as a university system has its own record on which to stand. The effectiveness of strategic planning depends on the intrinsic goals, objectives, and priorities identified—and their accomplishment on a reasonable schedule.

System and Process

Accepting the years 1990-2002 as twelve years in which the growth, progress, and/or development of the University System were unprecedented and asking the pertinent question, "Why, in Georgia?" the most plausible explanation is a fortuitous combination of executive leadership, a robust economy, and amazing opportunities that were alertly seized. Lending appreciable credibility to this explanation was the character and capabilities of Governor Zell Miller who was indeed favorably disposed to higher education because of his experience as faculty member at Young Harris College, his military training in the Marines, his sixteen years of service as lieutenant-governor, and his success in writing several well-received books. In 1965 when he withdrew to become an unsuccessful candidate for the U.S. Congress, he was a participant in the University of Georgia's Faculty Development Program, pursuing a doctoral degree in history.

Equally important, but in a different way, the appointment of Chancellor Stephen Portch and his energetic leadership must be "factored" into any interpretation or explanation of the University System's emerging visability and accomplishments. Chancellor Portch's educational history, experience, commitment, and timing may have been the most obvious "contributing factors" to the success of strategic planning while, at the same, being one of the most intangible. Whatever the "final equation" might disclose, the combination of Governor Miller's and Chancellor Portch's leadership will account for a highly significant *and* substantial portion of the systemwide changes between 1990-2001.

Taking for granted the fortunate opportunities created by the success of a state lottery, the national publicity given the use of lottery funds for college scholarships (Project HOPE), the selection of Atlanta as host for the 1996 Summer Olympics, and many other seemingly incidental events, the concurrence of favorable events suggests that success was likely, but not readily assured. Somewhat to the contrary, the fortunate circumstances of the University System's "windows of opportunity" conflicted to an appreciable degree with staunch efforts in the past to keep higher education as free as possible of "politics". As late as the spring of 2002, occasional newspaper articles condemned the use of lottery funds for scholarships on the grounds that such use was neither educationally sound nor morally appropriate.

Without implying that more profound reasons must be given to explain the University System's "emergence" as the nation's fourth largest statewide system of public higher education, there are many reasons that could be presented as quite relative and definitely supportive. Although less tangible than monetary returns on financial investments, the commitments and contributions of uncountable institutional leaders, faculty and staff members, students and graduates, sponsors and donors, and clients, users, employees, and visitors should be mentioned.

Among the other intangible but valuable contributions to the University System and the public interest are the indispensable contributions made by various administrators, faculty and staff members, and students who "learned from experience" and passed their experience along to others.

Although many planning processes begin with no sense of obligation to what previous planning committees or commissions have learned, no planning process begins with "a clean slate" or at "Square One" and develops a comprehensive plan worthy of the name. In higher education—every planning, self-study, and evaluation committee has been preceded by other committees, commissions, or councils who dealt with similar, if not identical, issues and problems—and arrived at conclusions and recommendations worthy of note.

With specific regard to the University System's planning process, many valuable precedents can be identified. It is not fanciful to regard the University System—"as a whole" and as a system of interrelated parts—as a "learning organization", with memories and intellectual resources, with certain attitudes, beliefs, and values and with particular goals, objectives, and preferences. If planning committee can discuss with ease their vision of the institution in the future, they can consider with reasonable objectivity the vision that their institution has facilitated, fostered, or encouraged in the past. It is not cynical to say that a university or university system without its own vision is dubiously worthy of its name.

Outcomes and Results

Viewing the University System of Georgia "as a united whole" and as "a complex system of interrelated parts", what can we say about its changing vision of itself during the 1990s. Neither the brilliance of a well-articulated vision nor the effectiveness of strategic planning can ensure that effective planning will result in a clearly stated vision—and visa versa, that well worded vision statements will serve as chart and compass in plotting paths through planning mazes. Indeed, we can say emphatically that a better articulated vision of the University System is (or should be) one of the most important outcomes of its strategic planning process.

There are excellent reasons to believe that the various planning processes of the past have been constructive learning experiences for the University System. Whatever we see, think, or believe about the University System, as an outcome of recent planning, has been influenced by the Governor's (Carl Sanders) Committee to Improve Education in the 1960s, the various Regents' Planning

Surveys of the 1960s and 1970s, the Governor's (George Busbee) Committee on Postsecondary Education in the late 1970s, and the Langdale Assessment of the University System in the 1980s. The participants of all past planning surveys and studies would agree that their particular efforts did not solve all the problems of higher education in Georgia, but the cumulative effect of all such efforts has advanced the cause and improved the quality of education beyond the high school. In other words, each committee or commission has contributed significantly to the University System's vision of itself in the opening years of a new century.

Looking Back on the years 1992-2001, it would seem most appropriate to attribute a significant portion of the University System's continuing development to the wisdom of delegating executive authority to a chancellor who serves the public interest while serving at the board's discretion. Just as the primary purpose of a board of trustees has been defined as "creating the most desirable presidency possible"—so should the primary purpose of the Board of Regents be "to make the Office of the Chancellor the most distinctive and honorable appointment in state government, education, and public affairs."

Another significant and substantial proportion of the University System's overall efforts and accomplishments should be attributed to the essential-but-uncounted commitments and contributions of the University System numerous constituencies— who must continue to learn from experience and who can, on appropriate occasions, speak with one voice. In all institutions, programs, and services—at all levels and in all areas—committed and competent leadership is essential. And if "teaching by example" is still good advice, so should "leading by example" be recognized and praised.

Looking Ahead to the year 2007, when another strategic planning process may be launched, it is not unseemly to take state, regional, and local pride in the University System of Georgia's many accomplishments—and to appreciate the fact that other states are watching Georgia's progress in higher education and seeking ways in which they can emulate the University System's "best practices" and learn more about the "combination of circumstances" from which Georgia has benefited. In the fall of 2002, the Senior Vice President for Academic Affairs and Provost at the University of Georgia was appointed President of Ohio State University. Among the reasons given in Ohio newspapers was a statement by the chancellor of the Ohio Board of Regents, "Georgia has been a case study of ours. They have one of the finest higher-education systems in the country."

All such results or outcomes are indicative of a remarkable change in public perceptions of the University System's status and accomplishments since the 1980s. The University System's vision of itself "as a whole" and as a well organized and effectively operating statewide system of public higher education is in full accord with its national recognition and status. In appraising, assessing, or judging the University System's performance in the years ahead, observers will appreciate more fully the continuing emergence or development of higher education as national, regional, and state resource for societal improvement and advancement, as well as a valuable resource in meeting state priorities. There is, as there should be, a healthy caution concerning the University System's role and responsibilities as "a fourth branch of government. And critics are not wrong in recognizing as a fact-of-life that academic integrity is often at risk when honors and ratings are mistaken for standards and achievement.

To Summarize: The many constituencies of the University System can indeed *look back* at challenges responsibly met and effectively managed. Much has been learned from the continuing efforts to establish realistic admission standards, to measure academic abilities and achievement, to address a host of access and equity issues, *and* to plan, organize and develop a three-tier system of public higher education that serves the needs and interests of a great majority of citizens and residents. In doing so, the faculties and staffs of its 34 institutions have waged a continuous campaign against careless preparation, indifferent commitment, and inert skills and competencies on the part of students who doubted either the value of education or their ability to succeed.

Participants, observers, and critics can *look ahead* and see many issues yet to be resolved. They can question the wisdom and the capabilities of public colleges and universities in solving societal problems that society has chosen *not* to solve. Cynics in their midst will call attention to solutions in the form of competitive commercialization, excessive privatization, and enthusiastic technocracy. A majority of the participants, however, could see opportunities and challenges not unlike those confronted in the

1990s—and they could respond with confidence that suitable solutions can be found, if sought in an objective, systematic, and reliable manner. And surely, some of the participants *looking ahead* will have learned from experience that there is much to learn from the experiences of others who have previously dealt with similar issues and difficulties.

When considered in their entirety, the instruction, public service and research programs of the 34 institutions substantiate and enhance the multiple purposes of public higher education. The development and effective use of human knowledge, competence, and understanding are indeed essential to the realization of individual and institutional purposes—and to the technological and cultural advancement of state and society.

In addition to their commendable physical facilities, faculties, students, programs, and services, the University System's institutions have many resources that are intangible but nonetheless essential to their continued development. Primary among such resources are the status and prestige of the Regents as a single, unified governing board for Georgia's institutions of higher learning. The formulation and coalescence of public and institutional policy for 34 institutions is a continuous challenge but it is a challenge for which the Board of Regents has commendable experience and a record of accomplishment. The public endorsement and reinforcement of the board's authority and responsibility, following political interference in the 1940s, is still an illustrative lesson in state politics. In similar manner, the many events accompanying or following the desegregation crises of the 1960s testify that Georgia's institutions of public higher education serve national and regional purposes as well as state, society, and community needs.

Institutional leadership is a public service that is often unappreciated. Within each institution of higher education, leadership often emerges to meet the crisis at hand. In turn, governing policies and decisions give guidance and direction to many institutional decisions and actions that are responsive and adaptive. Institutions of higher education thrive best when granted reasonable autonomy and freedom in the administration of internal processes, operations, and activities that do not require major policy decisions. In other words, leadership may often seem hesitant but institutional leaders often render public or community services that should not be taken for granted.

The University System's contributions—past, present, and potential—to state and society are too numerous to count, and the commitments of the Regents, chancellor and staff, and its thirty-four institutions to the intellectual, technological, and cultural advancement of individuals and institutions are commendable and exemplary. In both its contributions and commitments, the University System's experience in coping with various "recurrent issues" continues to be one of its valuable resources in successfully meeting challenges that must be met again and again.

Annotated Bibliography

Chapter One
Reorganization and Coordination: 1932-1943

Allen, Ivan (Chairman). Governor's Commission To Simplify and
Coordinate the Operations of Governmental Departments.
*Plan of Simplification and Coordination of the Departments,
Boards, Commissions, and Institutions of the State Government
of Georgia.* Atlanta: State of Georgia Executive Department,
1929.

The report that laid the legal-political groundwork for the
reorganization of state government during the Richard B.
Russell, Jr. administration. The chairman was a prominent
Atlanta businessman.

*Annual Reports from Regents of the University System of Geor-
gia: 1932-1989.*

Presented annually by the chairman of the Board of Regents
to the Governor. Early issues contain invaluable information
about the decisions and actions of the Board in establishing
the University System. Format and coverage were altered
somewhat with the 1964-1965 report and editorial style was
changed significantly in the late 1980s. Gives valuable data
on annual budgets, enrollments, and faculty.

Brittain, M.L. *The Story of Georgia Tech.* Chapel Hill: University
of North Carolina Press, 1948.

A history of Georgia Tech from the perspective of a president
emeritus. Brittain was president from 1922 to 1944 and was
quite familiar with the events of re-organization in 1932 and
the events of 1941-1942. Includes the complete act establishing the Board of Regents. Brittain was 78 years old when he
retired in 1944.

Brooks, Robert Preston. *The University of Georgia Under Sixteen
Administrations: 1785-1955.* Athens: University of Georgia
Press, 1956.

An administrative history of UGA by an active participant
who served as dean of business, dean of faculties, alumni

secretary, and director of two institutes. Gives a good account of the founding of the University System and a personal account of the "Cocking Affair." Also gives enrollment and financial data.

Candler, C. Murphey (Chairman). *Report of State Survey Committee.* Atlanta: State of Georgia Executive Department, 1925.

A Citizens Committee appointed by Governor Clifford Walker to survey "the condition and needs of our Educational System and institutions." The committee looked at the "common schools," A&M schools and junior colleges, and "the higher education institutions."

Coffman, L.D., Elliott, Edward C., Judd, Charles H., Zook, George F., and Works, George A. (Chairman). *Report to the Board of Regents of the University System of Georgia.* Atlanta: USGA, 1933.

The first of the statewide survey reports prepared by an outside group of experts is known as "the First Works Report."Contains valuable information about the early years of the Board of Regents and its responsibilities for units of the University System.

Cottingham, James A. *Patterns of Governance: A Study of the Establishment of the University System of Georgia, 1931-1943.* Doctoral Dissertation, University of Georgia, 1990.

A recent study of the University System's early years and the leadership of the Regents in decisions to close, merge, or reorganize the units inherited from their various boards of trustees. Also reviews the political events of 1941-1942.

Dorsey, Hugh M. (Governor and Chairman). *Report of Budget and Investigating Commission.* Atlanta: State of Georgia Executive Department, 1919.

Contains the earliest reference we have to a "State Board of Regents" for higher education and states the case for economies that would be effected by having only one board.

Dyer, Thomas G. *The University of Georgia: A Bicentennial History (1785-1985).* Athens: The University of Georgia Press, 1985.

An excellent interpretation of turning points in the University's history: the civil war and reconstruction, the rise of land-grant colleges, the creation of the Board of Regents, the merger of the agricultural and education colleges with the University, the "Cocking Affair," the enrollment of thousands of World War II veterans, and the University's desegregation in 1961.

Works, George A. (Director). *Report to the Board of Regents of the University System of Georgia 1943*. Atlanta: USGA, 1943.

The second survey report is known as "the Second Works Report." Funds for this study were acquired in 1940 but completion of the report was delayed by the University System's "time of troubles" in 1941-1942.

Chapter Two
Status and Authority: 1941-1945

Best, Jenny Warlick. *Characteristics and Activities of Georgia College and University Regents and Trustees*. Doctoral Dissertation, University of Georgia, 1988.

Provides interesting information on the individuals who serve as Regents in the University System of Georgia or as trustees for private colleges and universities within the state. Only ten of the fifteen Regents completed the survey instrument but at least three of the responding ten Regents also served on boards of trustees.

Board of Regents of the University System of Georgia. *The Policy Manual* (2nd ed.). Atlanta: USGA, 1982.

Supplemented monthly after each Regents meeting in which revisions in policy may have been made. Contains much useful information about the organization, administration, and governance of the University System and its various units.

Committee of the Southern Association of Colleges and Secondary Schools. *Report on University System of Georgia*. (December 3, 1941).

Summarizes the events leading up to the public hearing held in Atlanta and states succinctly the findings, conclusions, and recommendations of the committee. The committee report

is reprinted in its entirety in the *1941 Annual Report*; M.L.
Brittain's, *Story of Georgia Tech*; R.P. Brooks', *University of
Georgia*; and elsewhere.

Cook, James F., Jr. *Politics and Education in the Talmadge Era:
The Controversy over the University System of Georgia, 1941-
1942*. Doctoral Dissertation, University of Georgia, 1972.

An objective study of political interference in the affairs of
the University System and the best source of information about
some of the events of 1941-1942. Valuable for the interviews
conducted (in later years) with some of the active participants.

Gosnell, Cullen B. *Government and Politics of Georgia*. New
York: Thomas Nelson and Sons, 1936.

A general introduction to the politics, state government, and
economic issues of the 1930s. The author was an advocate of
better state government and an astute observer of state politics.

Orr, Dorothy. *A History of Education in Georgia*. Chapel Hill:
University of North Carolina Press, 1950.

Written by the granddaughter of Georgia's first (post-reconstruc-
tion) state school superintendent with valuable information
about the founding of Georgia's public school system, the
state's A&M schools, and institutions of higher education.
Contains biographical sketches of early educators.

Saye, Albert Berry. *A Constitutional History of Georgia*. Athens:
University of Georgia Press, 1948.

A thorough discussion of Georgia's several constitutions,
their contents and provisions, and the continuing need for
amendments and revisions.

Chapter Three
Expansion and Improvement: 1946-1960

Committee on Manpower and Education, *Special Reports*. Atlanta:
Governor's Conference on Education, 1959.

Four special reports dealing with: (1) testing, counseling, and guidance, (2) teacher education, (3) educational television, and (4) vocational-technical education. Each report was prepared by a task force appointed by the Georgia Nuclear Advisory Commission's committee on manpower and education. Useful for its consideration of needs and issues in each of the four areas.

McDonald, Thomas F. *An Investigation of the Effects of a Rapid Transition from "Open-Door" to "Selective" Admissions.* Doctoral Dissertation, Michigan State University, 1966.

A comparative study of Georgia State before-and-after its selective admissions program in 1959. Covers a six-year period in which the institution made radical revisions in its admission standards and altered its traditional mission and role. Changes in student characteristics were more evident than changes in faculty expectations and grading patterns.

Junior College Act of 1958. No. 53 (House Bill No. 686). *General Acts and Resolutions, Volume I: Georgia Laws 1958 Session.*

An act to provide for a system of junior colleges in Georgia and defining "junior college" as a community educational institution constructed and operated by a local operation authority (i.e., city, county, or independent school systems).

Pierson, Mary Bynum. *Graduate Work in the South.* Chapel Hill: University of North Carolina Press, 1947.

Contains valuable information about the late development of graduate education in southern universities. Includes useful information about graduate work at the University of Georgia, Emory, Mercer, and Georgia Tech, such as requirements for master's and doctoral degrees, growth of libraries, etc. The first two doctorates at the University of Georgia were conferred in 1940 (one in history and one in education).

Range, Willard. *The Rise and Progress of Negro Colleges in Georgia: 1865-1949.* Athens: University of Georgia Press, 1951.

An informative review of the development of colleges for blacks in Georgia, with good coverage of the institutions in the Atlanta University Complex, Paine College in Augusta,

and the three state colleges in Albany, Savannah, and Fort
Valley. Depicts the long struggle to overcome the neglect of
the state and the general public. Especially good in showing
the influence and support of philanthropists and foundations.

Strayer, George D. (Director). *A Report of a Survey of the University System of Georgia.* Atlanta: USGA, 1949.

The third survey conducted by outside experts since 1932;
contract was with George Strayer, former director of the Division of Field Studies of the Institute of Educational Research,
Teachers College, and thus, numerous references since 1949
to "the Strayer Report."

Chapter Four
Growth and Expansion: 1960-1972

Bowen, Joel Thomas, Jr. *Room To Grow: A Historical Analysis
of the Physical Growth at The University of Georgia: 1785-
1990.* Doctoral Dissertation, University of Georgia, 1990.

An informative study of the University of Georgia's physical
growth. Discusses the geographical and architectural development of the institution as it acquires new missions and
responsibilities. Relates the University's growth to that of
higher education within the state and nation.

Denning, Richard G. *A Study of Five Selected State-Supported
Four-Year Colleges which have Expanded from Junior Level
Institutions: An Analysis of Some Resulting Quantitative
Changes.* Doctoral Dissertation, University of Georgia, 1972.

An analysis of institutional changes as the result of escalation
from junior college to senior college status. Gives various
kinds of information on Augusta, Armstrong State, Columbus,
and Georgia Southwestern colleges. Includes Southern Tech,
a unit of Georgia Tech, that became a four-year college several
years later.

Fincher, Cameron. *Nursing and Paramedical Personnel In Georgia:
A Survey of Supply and Demand.* Atlanta: Georgia State College, 1962.

A thirteen-month study of twelve health professions in the state of Georgia. Employers were surveyed for vacancies, turnover, and future personnel needs; colleges and schools were surveyed for supply of personnel from educational and training programs.

Educating Georgia's People: Investment in the Future. Atlanta: Governor's Commission To Improve Education, 1963.

Final report of the commission appointed by Governor Carl Sanders in 1963. Excellent staff work and exceptional group of consultants, plus remarkable representation of the public interest by a blue-ribbon group, led to recommendations concerning statewide goals, planning, financing, and excellence at all levels of public education.

Martin, S. Walter. *A Role and Scope Study of the University System of Georgia.* (Unpublished manuscript, 1966).

Study prepared with staff assistance from the Institute of Higher Education. In 1966 Dr. Martin was vice chancellor of the University System and president-elect of Valdosta State College.

McGrath, Earl J. *The Predominantly Negro Colleges and Universities in Transition.* New York: Bureau of Publications, Teachers College, Columbia University, 1965.

An excellent study of the historically black colleges in the 1960s. Includes useful information about the institutions, their faculties, facilities, academic programs, and student services. Makes a strong case for institutional support as a national objective and in the public interest.

Regents Study on Community Junior Colleges in Georgia. Report to the Board of Regents. (Preliminary Draft, December 1964).

First draft of the committee's report in which recommendations for Bibb County-Houston County, Downtown Atlanta, West Atlanta, and South Atlanta areas were made. Includes detailed data on high school graduates, population growth, etc.

Simpson, George L., Jr. *A Dam Has Broken.* A Statement of Vital Interest to All Georgians by the Chancellor of the University System of Georgia. Atlanta: University System of Georgia, 1967.

A significant and influential discussion of the University System's need for additional public support in the days of its most rapid growth. The author was chancellor from 1965 to 1978.

System Summary. A Publication of the University System of Georgia.

A monthly summary of activities and events taking place in the University System. First issue was dated November 4, 1964; subsequent issues give particular emphasis to actions, decisions, policies of Regents and to changes in key personnel: Regents, chancellor's staff, presidents, and others. Was changed in 1990 to *The System Supplement,* a smaller, briefer publication.

Chapter Five
Reform and Consolidation: 1972-1984

Barth, Elizabeth A. *A Study of Academic Programs for Superior Students in Georgia Colleges and Universities.* Doctoral Dissertation, University of Georgia, 1981.

The status of academic programs designed to meet the needs of superior college students in Georgia. Includes the perspectives of directors and coordinators of programs for superior students in terms of program effectiveness and efficiency.

Boardman, Katherine B. *Employer Perceptions of Educational Outcomes from Georgia Colleges.* Doctoral Dissertation, University of Georgia, 1981.

A survey of employer satisfaction with the preparation of Georgia graduates and the extent of corporate participation in higher education considered appropriate for their organizations. Addresses the opportunities for participation in planning of educational programs.

Davis, Margaret C. *A Survey of Community Services Policies, Procedures, and Practices in Institutions of Higher Education in Georgia.* Doctoral Dissertation, University of Georgia, 1981.

The capability and commitment of public and private colleges in Georgia to respond to community educational needs and expectations. Survey found community service to be an objective of most colleges.

The Eighties and Beyond: A Commitment to Excellence. A Report of a Statewide Needs Assessment for Public Higher Education. Atlanta: Board of Regents, University System of Georgia, February 1983.

Based on a statewide needs assessment and identifying quality improvement, accessibility and centralization, effective delivery systems, leadership, productivity, and financial support as the state of Georgia's major needs. SEE ALSO *Assessment Resource Book*: Staff reports and collected data for Board of Regents' comprehensive statewide needs assessment initiated in 1981. (Atlanta: USGA, 1983).

Fincher, Cameron. *Planning For A Statewide System of Public Higher Education: Fifty Years of Trial, Error, and Eventual Success in Georgia.* Athens: Institute of Higher Education, University of Georgia, 1984.

A paper that covers many of Georgia's earlier efforts to adopt statewide planning for institutional and program development. Emphasizes the difficulties of statewide planning in the post-WWII years.

Fincher, Cameron. *Adult Learners and the SAT in the University System of Georgia.* Athens: Institute of Higher Education, University of Georgia, 1983.

An analysis of the academic performance of 1,694 adult learners in institutions of the University System. Defines adult learners as first-time freshmen who are over 24 years in age. Relates SAT scores and secondary preparation to college grades, age, gender, reasons for attending college, fields of study, and other indices of performance such as credits carried and credit earned.

Fincher, Cameron. "The Adversities of Success: The Responsibilities of Governing Boards in Meeting the Special Needs of Students." A paper presented at the annual meeting of the Association of Governing Boards in San Francisco in April 1984.

Discusses the responsibilities of governing boards for academic policies and standards that address the problems of educationally disadvantaged students. Programs in developmental studies at Savannah State and the University of Georgia are described as exemplary models within a context of system-wide policies.

Fincher, Cameron. *Uses of the SAT in the University System of Georgia.* (Report No. 86-5). New York: College Entrance Examination Board, 1986.

A survey of the frequency and effectiveness with which SAT scores are used in advisement and counseling, recruitment and admissions, academic and administrative decision making, research and planning, and developmental studies. Includes abstracts of doctoral dissertations, research reports, etc. dealing with the SAT and a meta-analysis of 26 years of SAT scores, high school averages, and college grades.

Formula For Excellence: Financing Georgia's University System in the '80s. Final Report of the Study Committee on Public Higher Education Finance. Atlanta: Office of the Governor, September 1982.

Recommends differentiated funding of institutions according to mission and functions. Universities, senior colleges, and junior colleges should be funded according to instructional productivity in five major program areas (humanities and social sciences; area studies and applied or professional fields; sciences and technological specialties; remedial/developmental education; and the professions of medicine, dentistry, and veterinary medicine).

Galvin, Marc A. *Policies and Practices for Transfer Credit and Credit-by-Examination in Georgia Postsecondary Institutions.* Doctoral Dissertation, University of Georgia, 1982.

A study of policies and practices concerning transfer credit and credit-by-examination in Georgia postsecondary institutions and how these procedures are instituted.

Governor's Committee on Postsecondary Education:

Postsecondary Issues: Action Agenda for the Eighties. Atlanta: COPE, 1979.

Report issued by the state's second 1202 commission as the result of its charge by Governor George Busbee to identify major problems, issues, and concerns confronting postsecondary education.

Georgia's Postsecondary Education in the Eighties: Goals and Objectives. Atlanta: COPE, 1980.

Second report issued by the Committee as the result of re-appointment and a charge by Governor Busbee to identify statewide goals and objectives in postsecondary education.

Georgia Postsecondary Education: Where We Are and Where We Need To Be. Atlanta: COPE, 1981.

The third report issued by the Governor's Commission on Postsecondary Education. Includes efforts to assess progress being made toward the state's postsecondary goals and objectives and reports progress in offering a diversity of institutions and programs, educational opportunities that serve student career needs, and cooperation among postsecondary institutions. Substantial progress was not being made, however, in public awareness, institutional responsiveness to educational needs, and adequate opportunities for a changing clientele.

Maintaining Progress in Georgia: Recommendations for Today and Concerns for Tomorrow. Atlanta: COPE, 1982.

Summarizes the committee's efforts to identify issues and problems, to identify statewide goals and objectives, and to assess achievement of educational goals. Recommends state policies for student financial aid, college admissions and remedial assistance, geographic access and program planning, and planning for future needs. Among recommendations is the establishment of a statewide advisory commission on postsecondary education.

Holbrook, Margaret W. *An Analysis of Policies and Programs for Increasing Student Retention in Institutions of Higher Education in Georgia.* Doctoral Dissertation, University of Georgia, 1981.

Surveys policies and programs in Georgia colleges for improving student retention. Describes differences in estimated retention rates which occur at public, private, two-year, and four-year colleges.

New State Directions for Postsecondary Vocational Education. Report of the Vocational Education Task Force (Robert B. Ormsby, Chairman). Atlanta: VETF, 1983.

Report of the task force appointed by Governor Joe Frank Harris to recommend new forms of governance for vocational education that would not require an independent state agency or constitutional authority.

Southern Regional Education Board:

Priorities for Postsecondary Education in the South. Atlanta: SREB, 1976.

Position statement by the SREB giving nine priorities for postsecondary education. Two priorities deal with statewide planning; four deal with needed curricular or program change in postsecondary institutions. The remaining three priorities deal with pervasive problems and issues that require the attention and concern of policy and decision makers at most levels of institutional and public action.

Within Our Reach. Report of the Commission on Goals for Higher Education in the South. Atlanta: SREB, 1961.

An exceptionally influential report that addressed the needs and opportunities for the development of higher education in the South. The goals stated are "optimal but reasonable" and decidedly within reach of the colleges and universities of the southern region.

Weast, Philip G. *A Profile of Interinstitutional Cooperation Among Public and Private Institutions of Higher Education in Georgia.* Doctoral Dissertation, University of Georgia, 1981.

A study of interinstitutional cooperation among three sectors of higher education in Georgia. Considers areas of cooperation and the effectiveness of cooperation; major reasons for institutional involvement in cooperation; and agencies, associations, and agreements through which most cooperation occurs.

Chapter Six
Review and Coordination: 1984-1992

Albright, John W. *High School Courses and College Performance: A Study of State-Mandated College Preparatory Curriculum Requirements for College Admission*. Doctoral Dissertation, University of Georgia, 1990.

Study was conducted on a sample of 426 freshmen at the University of Georgia and included statistical control of relevant background variables. Found a significant correlation between college grades and completion of the required preparatory curriculum.

Booth, Le-Quita R. *The University System of Georgia's Administrative Development Program: A Means To Increase The Pool of Black Administrators*. Doctoral Dissertation, University of Georgia, 1987.

Addresses the effectiveness of inservice development programs for academic administrators. Based on interviews with participating Regents Fellows, supervising administrators, presidents of participating institutions, and professional staff members who designed and implemented the program. Concludes that program objectives were effectively achieved but important personal and institutional expectations were not realized.

Burge, Lee, Fincher, Cameron, Hooper, John W., and Langdale, Noah. *A Report to the Chancellor: An Assessment of The University System of Georgia (1989)*. Presented to the Board of Regents of the University System of Georgia, 1989.

Report is the result of a two-year assessment of the University System at the request of Chancellor H. Dean Propst. The major thrust of the assessment team was to analyze the causes of difficulties in higher education, and to assess the course of its development.

Improving Undergraduate Teacher Education Programs in Georgia. Recommendations of the External Review Committee for the Improvement of Teacher Education in Georgia. Atlanta: University System of Georgia, 1986.

Report on the recommendations of an external review committee convened to consider teacher education, ways of improving teacher education programs, and actions or studies that should be undertaken. Contains forty-three recommendations for educating teachers.

Morris, Libby V. *Health Professions Personnel in Georgia.* Athens: Institute of Higher Education, University of Georgia, 1987.

A comprehensive statewide needs assessment involving health facilities, educational and training programs, and personnel in thirty-two health occupations. Although Georgia health care has improved significantly since the early 1960s, Georgia is still below the national average in most areas of health care.

Proposal for the Establishment of Regional Universities. Prepared by the Planning and Oversight Committee of the Board of Regents. Atlanta: University System of Georgia (September 13, 1989).

This committee report provides a framework for the consideration of regional universities within the University System. Included are organizational concepts and criteria by which regional universities should be approved. Contains the committee's recommendations and a proposed organizational chart for Georgia Southern University.

Roberts, Derrell C. (Chairman). *Mission and Role of Public Two-year Colleges in Georgia.* (Report of the Study Committee appointed by Chancellor H. Dean Propst in 1987).

A survey of the varied mission and roles of public two-year colleges, as perceived by their presidents and other institutional leaders. Documents at least five major roles that two-year colleges actively play in providing educational services to their constituencies.

Subcommittee on Academic Degree Program Assessment. *Academic Degree Program Assessment in the University System of Georgia: A Tentative Statement of Rationale, Purposes, and Procedures.* Prepared for the Administrative Advisory Committee (July 1977).

Foreshadows much of the later concern with the assessment of educational outcomes. Discusses problems of definition, measurement and assessment, purposes and expected outcomes of assessment, and the diversity of instruments and techniques available to program heads and other institutional leaders.

The University System of Georgia: Planning for the 1990s. Atlanta: Board of Regents of the University System of Georgia, 1990.

Report on a two-year, long-range planning study involving the 34 institutions of the University System. States the mission of the University System, its goals and objectives for the 1990s, and the institutional roles of universities, senior colleges, and two-year colleges. Based on consideration of demographic and economic trends, statewide and regional needs, and an assessment of needs in the major programs of the system. Recommendations address increased participation in higher education, strengthening the University System's role in economic development, coordinating institutional roles, and improving the quality of institutional programs and services.

Chapter Seven
Progress and Continuing Development: 1990-1998

Almanac of Higher Education 1991. Prepared by editors of the *Chronicle of Higher Education.* Chicago: University of Chicago Press, 1991.

An outstanding source of information on public and private higher education. Published annually as a special supplement in the *Chronicle* and then as a paperback volume for commercial distribution. Especially useful for its summary of national statistics and its profiles of the fifty states.

Carnegie Foundation for the Advancement of Teaching. *A Classification of Institutions of Higher Education*. Princeton: CFAT, 1987.

A functional classification of institutions in terms of educational level, degree programs, and resources. Classifies research universities, doctorate-granting institutions, comprehensive universities and colleges, and liberal arts colleges at two levels (I and II). Other classifications include two-year colleges, and professional institutions.

Fincher, Cameron and Bachtel, Douglas C. "Higher Education in Georgia: A System Profile." *Issues Facing Georgia* Series, Cooperative Extension Service, University of Georgia (June 1991).

A study of enrollments in public colleges and universities by county of student origin. Includes institutional enrollment patterns for universities, senior colleges, and two-year colleges as well as expenditures on higher education by state and local government.

Hudson, Cathy Mayes and Pounds, Haskin R. *Improving Preparation for College: The Effects of the College Preparation Curriculum On Academic Success in the University System of Georgia: 1988-1990*. Atlanta: Board of Regents of the University System of Georgia (June 1991).

An excellent summary of data collected in a study of the college preparation curriculum (CPC) approved by the Regents in 1984 for implementation in 1988. Provides data on institutions by subject matter field for the years 1988, 1989, and 1990. Concludes that the recommended high school curriculum is effective in preparing students for college but suggests that the percent of high school students completing the CPC is not increasing.

Information Digest 1989-1990: Public Higher Education in Georgia. Atlanta: Office of Research and Planning, University System of Georgia (April 1990).

An invaluable source of information on students, faculties, finances, and facilities within the University System. Includes general information on the University System and its institutions. First issued in 1984 and continued annually since that time.

Marks, Joseph L. *SREB Fact Book On Higher Education 1990.* Atlanta: Southern Regional Education Board, 1990.

The latest in a twenty-year series of factbooks giving comparable data and information on higher education in the SREB states. Includes comparable data for the nation and provides a profile of higher education in Georgia as well as other southern states. An excellent source of information since the early 1960s.

Marks, Joseph L. *Georgia: Public College and University Faculty Salaries Compared to National and SREB Averages: 1990-91.* Atlanta: Southern Regional Education Board, 1991.

An occasional report on faculty salaries in the public colleges and universities of Georgia. Comparisons are for full-time faculty members by institutional classification without regard for faculty rank or field of specialization. Other reports in the series deal with faculty salaries in other states.

Pounds, Haskin and Anderson, Robert S. *Normative Data for the 1989-1990 Freshman Class.* Atlanta: Office of Research and Planning, University System of Georgia, 1991.

The thirty-third issue of the University System's annual norms booklet for SAT scores, high school averages, and freshman grades. Printed in a new format with institutional profiles and norms that contain excellent information on the status and quality of public education in Georgia.

Chapter Eight
Continuing Progress and Maturity: 1994-2001

Fincher, Cameron. *University-Government and Academic Organization.* Reprint of paper presented at the Ninth European Association for Institutional Research Conference at the University of Twente in Enschede, the Netherlands (August 24, 1989).

Discusses similarities and differences in university-government relations in American, British, and Western European universities. Organizational similarities, as well as differences, are distinctive but often confusing. Emphasizes the uniqueness of American universities as opposed to governing and coordinating boards in other nations.

Fincher, Cameron. *Presidential Leadership and Institutional Mission.* Paper presented at 16th Annual EAIR Conference in Amsterdam (August 1994).

An informal case study of the university presidencies in the University System of Georgia. Observations and inferences concerning the distinctive but complementary missions of Georgia Technical Institute of Technology, Georgia State University, and the University of Georgia (i.e. their distinctive but complementary missions under the same governing board).

Libby V. Morris and Catherine J. Little, *Georgia's Health Professions: A Decade of Change 1985-1995.* Athens: University of Georgia, Institute of Higher Education, 1996.

The third report in a series of health profession studies in Georgia. Provides useful and interesting information about the development of health professions, the increasing demand for educational programs to prepare professional personnel, and the difficulties of increasing supply in response to rapid changes in specialized fields of health care.

Johnson, Sandra L. and Rush, Sean C. (Eds.). *Reinventing the University: Managing and Financing Institutions of Higher Education.* New York: John Wiley & Sons, 1995.

A comprehensive overview of challenges and issues in financing and managing higher education. Advocates the revitalization and/or the reinvention of universities by adopting "the best practices" of corporate finance and management. Addresses institutional programs, policy planning concepts and principles as the most efficient way of meeting growing demands for accountability—and presents thereby a significant contrast with planning methods and models in the past.

Katy, Richard N. and Associates. *Dancing with the Devil: Information Technology and the New Competition.* San Francisco: Jossey-Bass, 1999.

Discusses the changing environment in which institutions of higher education must meet the challenges of technological innovation in teaching and learning. Questions the survival of traditional methods of disseminating knowledge, information, and academic credentials in the midst of a "digital revolution" and intense competition from profit-driven organizations.

Keller, George. "Creating a Vision for the Future." In Johnson & Ruch (Eds.) *Reinventing the University.* New York: John Wiley & Sons, 1995, pgs. 381-390.

Provides a much-needed ballast for the enthusiastic emphasis on funding and financial reporting as the latest model in institutional planning. Reminds readers of other planning methods, regarded as incremental, transactional, or provisional that are deeply anchored in college and university histories.

Little, Catherine Joanne. *A Study of the Early Effects of the HOPE Grant at Public Colleges and Universities in Georgia.* Doctoral Dissertation, University of Georgia, 1995.

A commendable study of the benefits and difficulties in implementing the HOPE scholarships in its first two years, 1993-1994 and 1994-1995. Based on interviews with directors of student financial aid and directors of admissions, this doctoral dissertation was unusually timely and helpful in assessing the extent to which intended consequences were realized and in identifying various consequences that were unanticipated.

Sloop, Sue Lynn. *Keep a B and Go to College Free: An Examination of Grade Inflation.* Doctoral Dissertation, University of Georgia, 2000.

A thorough statistical analysis of "grade inflation" as affected by HOPE scholarships requiring the maintenance of a "B-average" for continuance in college. Reports a statistically significance increase in freshman grade-point averages following the awarding of HOPE Grants. Discusses the various implications of increased grade-point-averages for education and employment.

Richardson, Richard C., Bracco, Kathy Reeves, Callan, Patrick M., and Finney, Joni E. *Designing State Higher Education Systems for a New Century.* Phoenix: American Council on Education/Oryx Press, 1999.

A highly informative study of state roles and responsibilities in higher education governance. Discusses the performance and adaptability of statewide systems in Georgia, Florida, Texas, California, Illinois, Michigan, and New York—seven of the nation's ten most popular states. Excellent case studies of four state systems with multiple governing boards, two state systems with multiple governing boards and Georgia, as a unified system with constitutional authority.

Chancellor's Report to the Board of Regents (August 1999). *Where we started . . . Where we've been . . . Where we're going . . . A Review of the Board of Regents' Strategic Process: 1994-1999.*

A comprehensive overview and update on the University System's strategic planning process to date. Gives Chancellor Portch's professional and personal assessment of the progress during the first five years of strategic planning.

Chapter Nine
Continuing Commitment and Leadership: 2001-2002

Pappas Consulting Group, Inc., *University System of Georgia: Benchmarking and Management Review: Executive Summary.* (September 2000).

A comprehensive summary of the final reports for Project Scope I: Benchmarking Study concluded in September 2000 and Project Scope II: Management Review concluded in August 2000, studies commissioned by the Board of Regents in its effort to be fully accountable in meeting state priorities.

FY2002 Accountability Report: A report by the Board of Regents of the University System of Georgia to Governor Roy Barnes and the General Assembly relating progress to date on the special funding initiatives, capital projects and other key programs funded during the 2001 legislative session (February 2002).

A remarkably thorough report, as suggested by its subtitle, and an excellent status report on the progress made in the University System's implementation of it strategic planning process. Ninety-nine pages of financial and statistical information about the University System in its most challenging years of growth and development.

System Supplement: *A Report of the Georgia Board of Regents, Volume 38,* 2001 (various issues).

A valuable source of information during the year 2001 and representative of the Central Offices' efforts to keep faculties, students, and the general public informed about the numerous changes taking place with the University System.

Chancellor's Report to the Board of Regents, 2001 (various issues).

Another valuable source of information of interest to the 34 institutions, their faculties, and their staffs; of particular interest is Chancellor Portch's "State of the System" report in November 2001. Declaring " the state of the University System of Georgia has never been better" he assigned a grade of "A" to the Board of Regents for their vision and implementation of the system's strategic plan.

System Supplement: A Report of the Georgia Board of Regents, Volume 39, Number 5 (June 2002.)

Discusses Dr. Tom Meredith's inauguration as the tenth chancellor of the University System, former Governor Joe Frank Harris's election as chair of USGA's governing board, the adoption of an action plan for the first year of the Regents' new strategic plan, the positive findings of a systemwide study of student satisfaction, and the board's capital priorities for the next budget year.

Chancellor's Report to the Board. (Monthly, 2002).

Chancellor Thomas C. Meredith's first report to the Board of Regents in January and monthly reports to date. Comments, reports, and topics of interest presented to the Regents as deemed advisable.

Minutes of the Meeting of the Board of Regents of the University System of Georgia (June 11 and 12, 2002).

A highly informative "run through" of the University System's status and progress, as reflected in the transactions of the Board of Regents at the close of Fiscal Year 2002. Reflects the continuing progress made in the first five months of Chancellor Meredith's leadership.

Minutes of the Meeting of the Board of Regents of the University System of Georgia (August 6 and 7, 2002).

Includes the "Chairman's Remarks" by former Governor Joe Frank Harris who is current chair of the Board of Regents and identifies the three key areas on which the Regents will focus in Fiscal Year 2003. Primary emphasis is given to the first year action plan of the University System's revised strategic plan; secondary and tertiary will be placed on awareness of "the future" and educational partnerships, respectively. Includes also a highly informative presentation on the Skidaway Institute of Oceanography's strategic plan.

Minutes of the Meeting of the Board of Regents of the University System of Georgia (September 10 and 11, 2002).

Provides an interesting update on the Georgia Pubic Library Service (GPLS) and the progress made since its transfer to the University System in 2000. States the overall objective of GPLS as encouraging reading, literacy, and education through the continuing support and improvement of Georgia's public libraries. Discusses numerous other decisions and actions such as revised criteria for teaching faculty and approval of new degree programs. Also includes a report of the Strategic Planning Committee as a committee of the whole.

APPENDIX

The Constitutional Authority of the Board of Regents

The authority and responsibilities of the University System of Georgia Board of Regents derive from the Constitution of the State of Georgia, as revised and approved in the 1982 general election. The authority and powers granted by the State Constitution are as follows:

Paragraph I. University System of Georgia; board of regents.
(a) There shall be a Board of Regents of the University System of Georgia which shall consist of one member from each congressional district in the state and five additional members from the state at large, appointed by the Governor and confirmed by the Senate. The Governor shall not be a member of said board. The members in office on June 30, 1983, shall serve out the remainder of their respective terms. As each term of office expires, the Governor shall appoint a successor as herein provided. All such terms of members shall be for seven years. Members shall serve until their successors are appointed and qualified. In the event of a vacancy on the board by death, resignation, removal, or any reason other than the expiration of a member's term, the Governor shall fill such vacancy; and the person so appointed shall serve until confirmed by the Senate and, upon confirmation, shall serve for the unexpired term of office.

(b) The board of regents shall have the exclusive authority to create new public colleges, junior colleges, and universities in the State of Georgia, subject to approval by majority vote in the House of Representatives and the Senate. Such vote shall not be required to change the status of a college, institution or university existing on the effective date of this Constitution. The government, control, and management of the University System of Georgia and all of the institutions in said system shall be vested in the Board of Regents of the University System of Georgia.

(c) All appropriations made for the use of any or all institutions in the university system shall be paid to the board of regents in a lump sum, with the power and authority in said board to allocate and distribute the same among the institutions under its control in such way and manner and in such amounts as will further an efficient and economical administration of the university system.

(d) The board of regents may hold, purchase, lease, sell, convey, or otherwise dispose of public property, execute conveyances thereon, and utilize the proceeds arising therefrom; may exercise the power of eminent domain in the manner provided by law; and shall have such other powers and duties as provided by law. (e) The board of regents may accept bequests, donations, grants, and transfers of land, buildings, and other property for the use of the University System of Georgia.

(f) The qualifications, compensation, and removal from office of the members of the board of regents shall be as provided by law (*Constitution of the State of Georgia*, Article VIII, Section IV).

Index

About the Author

Cameron Fincher is one of many World War II veterans who would not have attended college without the G. I. Bill. In September 1946 he enrolled in the Day Division of the University System Center and since that time, with the exception of ten months while earning his master's degree, he has been either a student or a faculty member in the University System of Georgia. He was a student at the University System Center when it became the Atlanta Division of the University of Georgia and a faculty member when the Atlanta Division became Georgia State College.

His graduate degrees were earned at the University of Minnesota (MA, 1951) and Ohio State University (PhD, 1956) where he majored in psychology. In 1951 he was appointed instructor and counselor at the Atlanta Division where he taught psychology and established the Office of Testing and Counseling. In 1965 he transferred to the University of Georgia in Athens where he was first associate director (1965-1969) and then director (1969-1999) of the Institute of Higher Education. In 1980 he was designated Regents Professor of Higher Education and Psychology, and became the 10th UGA faculty member to hold the rank of Regents Professor. In his work at the Institute Dr. Fincher has actively participated in all phases of institutional and program planning, development, assessment, and evaluation.

In 1957 he was appointed to the first of many statewide or systemwide committees on which he has served. Since that time he has worked closely with the Board of Regents and other state agencies in the development and improvement of higher education in Georgia. From 1978 to 1983 he was a member of the Governor's Committee on Postsecondary Education, and from 1984 through 1988 he was actively involved in the organization and implementation of the Regents Administrative Development Program for minority faculty members. Over the years he has also worked closely with the Southern Regional Education Board, the Southern Education Foundation, the College Board, Educational Testing Service, the Southern Association of Colleges and Schools, and other regional or national agencies concerned with research and development in higher education.

His work has included service as a consultant to governing or coordinating boards in Alabama, Arkansas, Florida, Mississippi,

Louisiana, Tennessee, and South Carolina. His work has also been recognized by awards from the Association for the Study of Higher Education, the Association for Institutional Research, the Georgia Association for Institutional Research, Planning, Assessment, and Quality, the College Board, and resolutions by the Georgia Assembly.

The author's interest in the historical development of the University System began in the early 1950s when its central offices were located in the same building with the Atlanta Division. That interest continues to be whetted by numerous opportunities to explain the University System to doctoral students in higher education, to visiting educators from other countries—and to recently appointed faculty colleagues across campus.

About the Institute

The Institute of Higher Education was established in 1964 in response to the Southern Regional Education Board's recommendation that one or more universities in the region should establish a center or institute for the study of higher education. The Institute's original charges were: to help recruit and develop faculty members for institutions of higher education in Georgia, to conduct institutional studies for the University of Georgia, and to cooperate with other educational agencies and institutions in the development of higher education within the state and the region.

The Institute staff is actively involved in many projects and activities related to the overall development of higher education and to the improvement of institutions, programs, and services. Closely related to all Institute activities is a doctoral program specifically developed for the study of undergraduate, graduate, and professional education. In addition to the doctoral program the Institute staff has maintained a special interest in administrative leadership, faculty development, instructional improvement, program assessment, and the legal issues of American higher education. More recently the mission of the Institute includes commitment to the continuing professional education of academic administrators, professional staff members, and college teachers.

Throughout its thirty-eight years of service, the Institute has continued to work closely with the Southern Regional Education Board and other national or regional organizations concerned with the development of higher education. In particular, the Institute has worked closely with the Board of Regents, the chancellor's staff, and other state agencies dealing with the improvement of education in Georgia. Professional staff members have been involved in cooperative efforts with numerous institutions and associations seeking ways in which they can assist others in meeting the many challenges of changing public demands and expectations. Institute programs, services, and activities have been recognized nationally, regionally, and oncampus for their systematic and effective contributions to the continuing development of higher education.

Quotes from the decades . . .

"Our aim is to encourage diversity of educational effort because of the diversity of human needs. . . . It is essential that local pride must give way to the best educational interests of the whole State."   —*1932 Annual Report*

"We are convinced that we must be prepared for a greatly enlarged attendance when hostilities have ceased, and all temporary programs were necessarily conducted with this outlook in mind."   —*1944 Annual Report*

"Several factors are tending to produce a decline in enrollment. . . . Many veterans are completing their courses of study . . . Then, too, the outbreak of hostilities in the Far East has resulted in a demand for an increase in the armed forces. . . . The war effort of the country has created many new jobs in business and industry. . . . Most of our public schools are now in a process of transition from an eleven to a twelve grade program."   —*1950 Annual Report*

"This has been a year of much expansion and progress in the University System, in the physical facilities of the institutions, in student enrollments, in number of faculty members, in curricula and programs, and in financial support. . . . The Board of Regents approved the offering of six new Ph.D. programs and . . . thirty new baccalaureate degree programs."   —*1964 Annual Report*

"The 28 University System institutions in operation in 1972-73 were both individually distinctive and mutually dependent and inter-related. They were geographically dispersed so that more than 90 percent of the population of the state of Georgia resided within 35 miles of at least one of the campuses."   —*1973 Annual Report*

"The 1985-1986 year marked the achievement of one of the University System's primary goals—full funding of our 'formula for excellence.'"   —*1986 Annual Report*

"Still there is much work to be done. We can ill afford to slow the momentum or rest on our laurels. If we do, the investment that's been made will be wasted; we will quickly slide into being average—and that's not good enough for Georgia."   —*1998 Annual Report*